A · SHORT · COURSE · IN PHOTOGRAPHY

REVISED EDITION

· A Guide to Great Pictures ·

Carl Fleischhauer

· BARBARA LONDON ·

Curtin & London, Inc.
Somerville, Massachusetts

Van Nostrand Reinhold Company
New York   Cincinnati   Toronto   Melbourne

Printed in the United States of America

Published in 1983 by Curtin & London, Inc. and Van Nostrand Reinhold Company 135 West 50th Street, New York, NY 10020, U.S.A.

Van Nostrand Reinhold Limited
1410 Birchmount Road
Scarborough, Ontario M1P 2E7, Canada

Van Nostrand Reinhold Pty. Ltd.
17 Queen Street
Mitcham, Victoria 3132, Australia

Acknowledgments

Thank you to those organizations who granted us permission to reproduce the photographs on the following pages: Bethlehem Steel, 103 (bottom); EPA - Documerica, 5 (top), 24, 29 (top), 59, 63 (top), 72, 82, 85, 103 (top); Library of Congress American Folklife Center, i, 9 (center), 67 (bottom), 84, 99, 109 (bottom), 113 (top and bottom, left), 115 (top and bottom, right); National Park Service, 9 (top), 28, 32, 50, 63 (bottom), 67 (top), 69 (bottom), 71 (bottom), 74, 97 (top); U.S. Department of Agriculture, 22, 23, 26, 34 (top), 38, 43 (top and bottom), 44, 45, 49, 52 (top and bottom), 57, 62, 66, 70 (right), 73, 87 (top left, top right, and bottom), 96, 101, 104, 105 (top and bottom), 107 (top and bottom), 110 (left), 111 (top), 112 (top), 113 (bottom right), 115 (bottom left).

Cover design and interior design: Richard Spencer
Cover photograph: Laura Zito
Illustrations: Carol Keller
Production editor: Alison Fields
Composition: Jay's Publishers Services, Inc.
Printing and binding: Halliday Lithograph
Color insert printed by: Phoenix Color Corp.

Library of Congress Cataloging in Publication Data

London, Barbara
  A short course in photography.

  Includes index.
  1. Single-lens reflex cameras.   2. Photography— Handbooks, manuals, etc.   I. Title.
TR261.U67 1983   770'.28'22   83–5271
ISBN 0–930764–51–X

10 9 8 7 6 5 4 3 2 1

· CONTENTS ·

Olympus Camera Corp.

· CHAPTER 1 ·

Vivitar Corp.

· CHAPTER 2 ·

Gordon Baer

· CHAPTER 3 ·

Film and exposure · 38

· CHAPTER 4 ·

Color · 60

Fred Ward

Special techniques · 72

· CHAPTER 5 ·

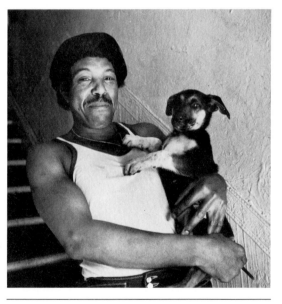

Jonas Dovydenas

Lighting · 84

· CHAPTER 6 ·

· CHAPTER 7 ·

Seeing like a camera · 96

Olympus Camera Corp.

Guide to equipment and accessories · 116

· PREFACE ·

Camera controls—f-stops, shutter speeds, focal length of lenses, focusing—can initially appear to be very complicated. But if you have just bought or are contemplating the purchase of a modern 35mm single-lens-reflex camera, all that you need to know to begin taking good pictures can be learned in a weekend and probably on a Saturday afternoon. The key is that the basic principles that take this short amount of time to learn have an almost infinite variety of combinations and it is those combinations that make photography both interesting and an avocation with a lifetime of possible growth.

Photography isn't as difficult as it used to be. The innovations in equipment make it much easier to get good exposures in all kinds of lighting situations. The introduction of new materials and electronic technology, particularly computer circuitry, have made possible a new generation of cameras—simple to operate, compact, and versatile. Today, you can master the basics much faster, so you can concentrate on what is important . . . the image.

This book covers the basic principles of photography, the ones that must be understood to take full advantage of the creative controls on the camera you use. Essentially you need to know how to obtain a good exposure and how to use focus, aperture (the size of the lens opening), and shutter speed to create the picture you want. These basic principles are stressed and presented completely. In addition, the book covers film, flash, exposure meters, accessory equipment, and other important information.

The book is designed so that every two facing pages complete a fundamental idea. This format permits you to use the book as a reference and to learn about specific topics as the need arises. The book is heavily illustrated with photographs and line art so that it can be understood more easily and quickly. It has been completely revised and updated in this brand-new edition to bring you the latest information on camera equipment and accessories.

There is no doubt that greater satisfaction comes from using the camera as a creative tool and it is toward that end that this book will lead. ▪

Chapter 1
· CAMERA ·

Olympus Camera Corp.

If you have progressed beyond the stage of simply wanting to take ordinary snapshots, then the 35mm single-lens-reflex (SLR) will probably be the camera you choose. It is small enough to carry almost anywhere, yet it uses film large enough to produce prints and slides of good quality. The special features and great flexibility of the SLR make it popular with professional photographers, with people who are seriously interested in photography, and with those who like to take pictures just for the fun of it.

Through-the-lens viewing A single-lens-reflex uses the same lens both for viewing the scene and for exposing the film, so what you see in the camera's finder is a good indication of what you'll get in the final picture. SLR cameras with built-in exposure meters make light readings directly through the lens, which means that you can also see exactly which area or object is being metered.

Automation In just the last few years a revolution has occurred in camera design. In many models one of the major controls in picture making—exposure—has been taken over by tiny silicon chips and other components built into the camera. This electronic circuitry measures the light and then lets in just enough to expose the film properly. In some cases you will want to (and you usually can) override the decision of these automatic calculators, but in many situations they will expose your picture so well that all you have to do is focus and shoot. And for the maximum in automation, some cameras will confirm your focus or even focus automatically for you.

(A) pocket camera
(B) twin-lens-reflex
(C) 35mm single-lens-reflex
(D) 35mm range finder
(E) 4 x 5 view camera
(F) large format single-lens-reflex

Compact size When you hold a 35mm single-lens-reflex camera in your hands, it feels comfortable—compact and convenient to carry with you. SLRs are getting even smaller and lighter as electronic circuitry replaces the maze of springs and gears that used to power shutters and other mechanisms.

Versatility When you buy an SLR, you are buying a system, not just a camera. Lenses are interchangeable, and in many models other parts are as well. Options like automatic flash units and motor-driven film advance are available.

This book describes what SLRs do and how you can use their special features to make the pictures you want. ▪

THE SINGLE-LENS-REFLEX:
BASIC CREATIVE CONTROLS

Cameras don't quite "see" the way the human eye does, so at first the pictures you get may not be the ones you expected. One of the aims of this book is to help you gain control over the picture-making process by showing you how to see more the way the camera does and how to use the camera's controls to make the pictures you want. ∎

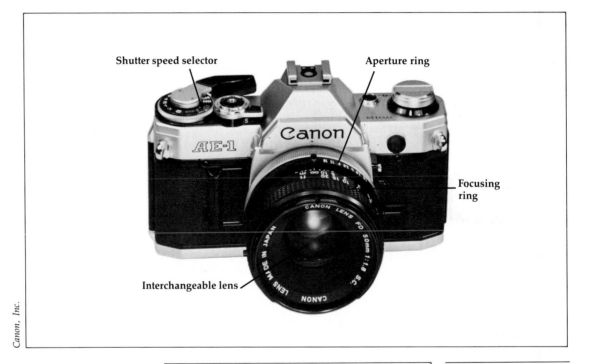

Shutter speed selector

Aperture ring

Focusing ring

Interchangeable lens

Canon, Inc.

Nikon, Inc.

◀ **Interchangeable lenses** With a single-lens-reflex you can make a picture with a lens of normal focal length—a lens that views a scene just about as you do. Or, since you can carry several lenses with you and change them as you wish, you can get very different pictures of the same scene—a greatly enlarged image of a distant object, for example. See opposite, bottom and pages 20–27 for more about focal lengths. ▶

Fred Ward

Focusing Through the viewfinder window you see the scene that will be exposed on the film, including the sharpest part of the scene, which is the part the camera is focusing on.

A particular part of a scene can be focused sharply by turning the focusing ring on the lens. More about focusing and sharpness appears on pages 12–15 and 30–33.

Alan Oransky

Shutter speed control Objects that are moving can be shown dead sharp and frozen in mid-motion or blurred, either a little bit or a lot. Turn to pages 10–11 and 14–15 for information about shutter speeds, motion, and blur.

Fredrik D. Bodin

Aperture control Do you want part of the picture sharp and part out of focus, or do you want the whole picture sharp from foreground to background? Changing the size of the aperture (the lens opening) is one way to control this. More about aperture on pages 12–15.

Alan Oransky

INSIDE A 35mm
SINGLE-LENS-REFLEX

The lightweight, compact body of a modern single-lens-reflex camera is sleek and functional. If you could cut away the shell of your SLR, you'd find packed inside thousands of precisely engineered mechanical and electronic parts. All of them are there to help you take better pictures—by making the camera easy to operate, critically accurate in focusing and other controls, and rugged enough to be reliable day after day. Below is a simplified look inside a single-lens-reflex (designs vary in different models). The camera takes its name from its single lens (some reflex cameras have two lenses) and from its reflection of light upwards for viewing the image. ▪

The shutter of a single-lens-reflex camera is located just in front of the film (at L in the camera diagram). During exposure the shutter opens to form a slit that moves across the film. The size of the slit is adjustable; the wider the slit, the longer the exposure time and the more light that reaches the film. Shown here is a shutter that travels horizontally across the film. Some shutters travel vertically.

Inside a single-lens-reflex (opposite)

A. Body The light-tight box that contains the camera's mechanisms and protects the film from light until you are ready to make an exposure.

B. Lens Focuses an image on the film. Single-lens-reflex lenses are interchangeable.

C. Lens elements The optical glass lens components that produce the image.

D. Focusing ring Turning the ring focuses the image by adjusting the distance of the lens elements from the film plane.

E. Iris diaphragm A circle of overlapping leaves that open up to increase (or close down to decrease) the amount of light reaching the film.

F. Aperture ring Turning the ring adjusts the size of the iris diaphragm inside the lens.

G. Mirror During viewing, the mirror reflects light from the lens upwards onto the viewing screen.

H. Viewing screen A ground-glass (or similar) surface on which the focused image appears upside down and backwards. Some SLR cameras have interchangeable viewing screens with cross lines or other features.

I. Pentaprism A five-sided optical device that reflects the image from the viewing screen until it appears right side up and correct from left to right. On some cameras the pentaprism can be replaced with a specialized viewfinder such as a waist-level finder.

J. Metering cell Measures the brightness of the scene being photographed.

K. Viewfinder eyepiece A window in which the corrected image from the pentaprism is visible to the photographer.

L. Shutter During an exposure, the mirror first swings upwards out of the way so the light passes straight ahead. Then the shutter opens to expose the film to the light. Shutter action is diagrammed opposite at top.

M. Film The light-sensitive material that records the image.

N. Film advance A lever that advances an unexposed segment of film behind the shutter in preparation for exposure.

O. Shutter speed dial Selects the shutter speed or, in some models, the mode of automatic exposure operation.

P. Shutter release A button that activates the exposure sequence in which the mirror rises, the shutter opens, and the film is exposed.

Q. Hot shoe A bracket that attaches a flash unit to the camera and with suitable units provides the electrical linking that synchronizes the camera and the flash.

R. Rewind mechanism A crank that rewinds the film into its cassette after the roll of film has been exposed.

S. Film cassette The light-tight container in which 35mm film is packaged.

SINGLE-LENS-REFLEX ELECTRONICS

As cameras become more complex internally, incorporating sophisticated computing modules and other electronic devices, they are actually becoming *less* complicated for the photographer to use. One of the advantages of the new camera electronics is that you can spend more time concentrating on the people or location you are photographing and less time making exposure readings and calculations.

You have a choice of automatic exposure modes with some cameras, like the one shown below. In shutter-priority mode, you set the shutter speed and the camera automatically sets the correct aperture (lens opening). This mode is useful when the motion of subjects is important, as at sporting events, because the shutter speed determines whether moving objects will be sharp or blurred.

In aperture-priority mode, you set the lens opening and the camera automatically sets the shutter speed. This is useful when you want to control the depth of field or sharpness of the image from foreground to background, because the size of the lens opening is a major factor affecting sharpness.

With programmed operation, the camera selects both the shutter speed and the aperture based on a program built into the camera by the manufacturer. This automatic operation can be useful in photographing fast-moving subjects because it allows you to simply focus and shoot.

Manual operation is also a choice with many automatic cameras. You set both the lens opening and shutter speed yourself, using, if you wish, the camera's built-in light meter to measure the brightness of the light. More information about camera choices begins on page 122.

But even with automatic operation you have flexibility in exposure choices. For example, in aperture-priority operation, you can change the shutter speed too; you can shoot at a faster shutter speed by opening the aperture wider, or at a slower speed by making the aperture smaller. The aperture is similarly adjustable when you are in shutter-priority operation. ∎

A modern compact automatic, 35mm single-lens-reflex camera—the Minolta X-700. Among the camera's exposure modes are aperture-priority automatic, programmed automatic, and manual.

Minolta Corp.

Motor drive units advance and expose film with one push of a button. Some units can capture sequences of photographs at speeds up to 5 frames per second, make multiple exposures on the same frame or expose film a single frame at a time. If you don't have to pause to advance the film, you get a few extra seconds—sometimes critical ones—to adjust the focus or framing. ▶

5.6

Exposure information appears in the camera's viewfinder so you never have to lose sight of your subject to make exposure adjustments. This viewfinder shows the preselected shutter speed and/or aperture. Light-emitting diode (LED) readouts show shutter speed or aperture settings that are set automatically. This viewfinder also features LED displays to show you when the flash is ready to fire and to give you warnings of under- or overexposure.

Some cameras provide confirmation that the image is in focus. Here, the small frame in the middle of the viewfinder screen is centered on the object. When the shutter release button is pressed halfway down, one of three signals lights up on the lower edge of the viewfinder. Red arrowheads warn you if the image is out of focus and show you which way to turn the lens to focus it sharply. A green circle lights up when the image is sharp.

Terry Eiler

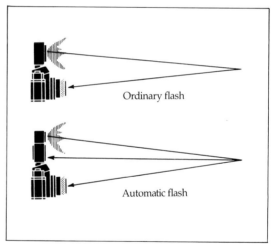

Ordinary flash

Automatic flash

◀**For flash pictures,** automatic flash units read the light reflected back from the subject and cut off the flash at the proper exposure. Some recycle fast enough to be used with motor drive units.

Fredrik D. Bodin

SHUTTER SPEED:
AFFECTS LIGHT AND MOTION

Light and the shutter speed The shutter is one way to control the amount of light that strikes the film. (The aperture, page 12, is the other.) The shutter speed dial on the camera sets the shutter so it remains open for a given fraction of a second after the shutter release is pressed (see illustration below). The B, or bulb, setting keeps the shutter open as long as the shutter release is held down.

Motion and the shutter speed In addition to controlling the amount of light that enters the camera, the shutter speed also affects the way that moving objects are shown. A fast shutter speed can freeze motion—from a ballet leap to a falling drop of water. A slow shutter speed keeps the lens open long enough for the image to blur. The important factor is how much the image actually moves across the film. The more of the film it crosses while the shutter is open, the more the image will be blurred. The shutter speed needed to freeze motion depends in part on the direction in which the subject is moving in relation to the camera (see opposite).

The focal length of the lens and the distance of the subject from the camera also affect the size of the image on the film and thus how much it will blur. A subject can appear small if it is photographed with a short-focal-length lens or if it is far from the camera, and so it may move relatively far before its image crosses enough of the film to be blurred.

Obviously, the speed of the motion is also important, and, all other things being equal, a darting swallow needs a faster shutter speed than a hovering hawk. Even a fast-moving subject, however, may have a peak in its movement, when the motion slows just before it reverses. A gymnast at the height of a jump, for instance, or a motorcycle on a sharp curve is moving slower than at other times and so can be sharply photographed at a relatively slow shutter speed.

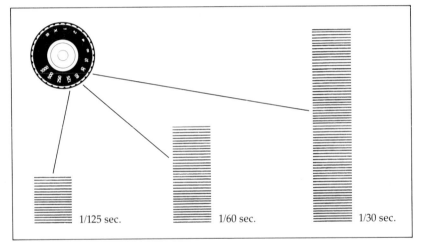

1/125 sec. 1/60 sec. 1/30 sec.

Shutter speed settings are typically in seconds: 1 sec., 1/2 sec., 1/4, 1/8, 1/15, 1/30, 1/60, 1/125, 1/250, 1/500, 1/1000, and sometimes 1/2000 and 1/4000. Only the bottom part of the fraction appears on the shutter speed dial and in any exposure information displayed in the viewfinder. Each setting lets in twice as much light as the following setting (or half as much as the previous setting): 1/60 sec. lets in twice as much light as 1/125 sec., half as much as 1/30 sec.

Blurring to show motion Freezing a motion is one way of representing it, but not the only way. In fact, freezing a motion sometimes eliminates movement altogether so that the subject seems to be at rest. Allowing the subject to blur can be a graphic means of showing that it is moving.

Panning to show motion Panning the camera—moving it in the same direction as the subject's movement during the exposure—is another way of showing motion (bottom right). The subject will appear sharper than it would if the camera were held steady, while the background will be blurred. ▪

1/30 sec.

1/125 sec.

Slow shutter speed, subject blurred The direction a subject is moving in relation to the camera can affect the sharpness of the

picture. At a slow shutter speed, a jogger moving from left to right is not sharp.

Fast shutter speed, subject sharp Photographed at a faster shutter speed, the same jogger moving in the same direc-

tion is sharp. During the shorter exposure her image did not cross enough of the film to blur.

1/30 sec.

1/30 sec.

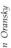

Slow shutter speed, subject sharp Here the jogger is sharp even though photographed at the slow shutter speed that recorded blur in the

first picture. Because she was moving directly toward the camera, her image did not cross enough of the film to blur.

Panning with the jogger is another way to keep her relatively sharp. During the exposure the photographer moved the

camera in the same direction that the jogger was moving.

Alan Oransky

APERTURE: AFFECTS LIGHT AND DEPTH OF FIELD

Light and the aperture The aperture, or lens opening, is another control that you can use in addition to shutter speed to adjust the brightness of the light that reaches the film. Turning a ring on the outside of the lens changes the size of the aperture diaphragm, a ring of overlapping metal leaves inside the lens. Like the iris of your eye, the diaphragm can get larger (open up) to let more light in; it can get smaller (stop down) to decrease the amount of light.

Light and the aperture The size of the lens opening—the aperture—controls the amount of light that passes through the lens. Each aperture is one "stop" from the next, that is, each lets in twice as much light as the next smaller opening, half as much light as the next larger opening. Notice that the smaller the lens opening, the larger the numeral. F/22 is a smaller opening than f/16, which is smaller than f/11, and so on.

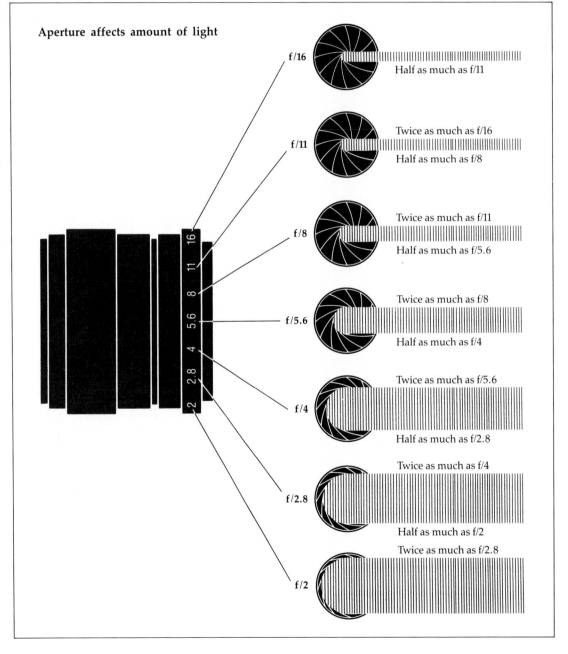

Aperture affects amount of light

f/16 — Half as much as f/11

f/11 — Twice as much as f/16 / Half as much as f/8

f/8 — Twice as much as f/11 / Half as much as f/5.6

f/5.6 — Twice as much as f/8 / Half as much as f/4

f/4 — Twice as much as f/5.6 / Half as much as f/2.8

f/2.8 — Twice as much as f/4 / Half as much as f/2

f/2 — Twice as much as f/2.8

Aperture setting (f-stops) These are: f/1 (theoretically the widest opening), f/1.4, f/2, f/2.8, f/4, f/5.6, f/8, f/11, f/16, f/22, f/32, f/45. F-stops smaller than f/45 are seldom found. Each aperture setting lets in twice as much light as the next setting up the scale (or half as much light as the next setting down the scale). The relationship is not as obvious from the sequence of f-stop numbers as it is with shutter speeds (which also have a half-or-double relationship: 1 second, ½ second, ¼ second, and so on), but after a while the f-stops become just as familiar and easy to remember. No lens has the entire range of f-settings. A 50mm lens may range from f/2 to f/16, a 200mm lens from f/4 to f/22.

One irregularity sometimes occurs: the widest f-stop may be slightly less or slightly more than one full stop from the next setting. For example, a lens may open to f/3.5, then go to the regular sequence of f/4, f/5.6, and so on.

Depth of field and the aperture The size of the aperture setting also affects the relative sharpness of objects in the image, known as depth of field. In theory, only one distance from the lens, the plane of critical focus, can be acutely focused at one time. However, in practice, part of the scene near the plane of critical focus also appears acceptably sharp. As the aperture opening gets smaller, the depth of field increases and more of the scene appears sharp in the photograph. (More about depth of field on pages 30–33.) ▪

Aperture affects depth of field

Fredrik D. Bodin

Depth of field and the aperture The larger the aperture opening, the less the depth of field. At f/16 (above) the entire depth in the scene from foreground to background was sharp. At a much larger aperture, f/2 (below), the depth of field decreased considerably so that only the third cannon from the front, on which the photographer focused, is completely sharp.

SHUTTER SPEED AND APERTURE: BLUR VS. DEPTH OF FIELD

Controlling the amount of light
There are two controls over the amount of light striking the film: shutter speed (length of exposure) and aperture (brightness of light). Either one can be used to increase or decrease the amount of light.

Each f-stop setting lets in half (or double) the amount of light as the adjoining setting. Each shutter speed setting does the same. A move to the next setting changes the exposure by one stop. Correct exposure can be obtained from any combination of f-stop and shutter speed settings that lets in the proper amount of light. The exposure stays constant if, for example, a move to the next faster shutter speed (minus one stop exposure) is matched by a move to the next larger aperture (plus one stop exposure).

Other effects on the image But since the shutter speed also affects the way motion is shown and the size of the aperture also affects the overall sharpness of the photograph (its depth of field), you can decide for each picture whether stopped motion or depth of field is more important. More depth of field (with a small aperture) means more possibility of blur (with a slow shutter speed) and vice versa. Depending on the situation, you may have to compromise on a moderate amount of depth of field with some possibility of blur. ▪

Shutter speed and aperture combinations Both the shutter speed and the aperture size control the amount of light that strikes the film. Each setting lets in half (or double) the amount of light as the adjacent setting. In manual exposure operation (where you set both the shutter speed and aperture), changing from one setting to the next changes the exposure by one stop, so if you decrease the amount of light one stop by moving to the next smaller f-stop setting, you can keep the exposure constant by also moving to the next slower shutter speed.

In automatic exposure operation, the camera makes these adjustments for you. For example, if you change the aperture, the camera automatically changes the shutter speed to keep the exposure constant.

Each combination of f-stop and shutter speed shown lets in the same amount of light, but, as illustrated at right, different f-settings and shutter speeds change the depth of field and appearance of motion in the picture.

Fredrik D. Bodin

Shutter speed and aperture combinations

Each of the combinations for the scene at left let in the same total amount of light, so the overall exposure stayed the same. But the people sledding are less or more blurred depending on whether a fast or slow shutter speed was used. And the depth of field (overall sharpness of nonmoving objects) is greater or smaller depending on whether a small or large aperture was used.

Very fast shutter speed (1/1000 sec.): the sled and rider are sharp. **Very wide aperture** (f/2): the people in the background are definitely out of focus.

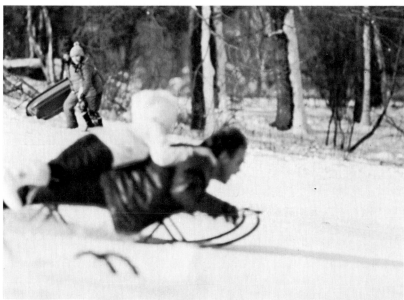

Medium-fast shutter speed (1/125 sec.): the moving sled is slightly blurred. **Medium-wide aperture** (f/5.6): the background is sharper than above.

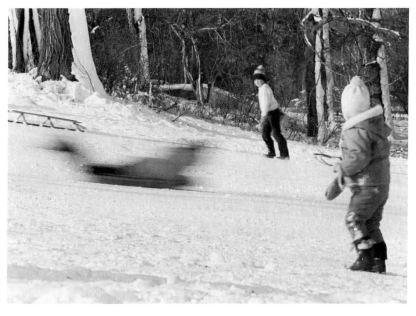

Slow shutter speed (1/15 sec.): the sled is very blurred because of its motion during the exposure. **Small aperture** (f/16): the trees are distinctly sharp; compare the branches to the picture above.

CARE OF
CAMERA AND LENS

Cameras are remarkably sturdy instruments considering the precision mechanisms that they contain, but a reasonable amount of care in handling and maintaining a camera will more than repay you with longer trouble-free life and better performance.

To protect a camera in use, try a neck strap, either worn around your neck or wound around your wrist. It keeps the camera handy and makes you less likely to drop it. Eveready cases enclose the camera and have a front that folds down for picture taking. They provide protection but can be tedious to take off and put on. Gadget bags are good for carrying extra items. Lenses can be kept in plastic bags to protect them from dust, with lens caps both back and front for additional protection of lens surfaces. Aluminum cases with fitted foam compartments provide the best protection against jolts and jars; their disadvantage is that they are not conveniently carried on a shoulder strap. In a high-theft area, some photographers prefer a case that doesn't look like a camera case—for example, a sports bag or a small backpack. A beat-up case that looks as though it contains sneakers and a sweatsuit is less likely to be stolen than one that shouts "cameras."

Battery power is essential to the functioning of most cameras. If your viewfinder display begins to fail or act erratically, the batteries may be getting weak. Many cameras have a battery check that will let you test battery strength; it's a good idea to check batteries before beginning a day's shooting or a vacation outing and to carry

spares in your camera bag. If you don't have spares and the batteries fail, try cleaning the ends of the batteries and the battery contacts in the camera with a pencil eraser or cloth; the problem may just be poor contact. Warming the batteries might also bring them back to life temporarily.

Cameras and film in transit should be protected from excessive heat; for example, avoid putting them in a glove compartment on a hot day. Excessive heat not only affects the quality of film, it can soften oil in the pores of metal in the camera, causing the oil to run out and create mischief such as jamming lens diaphragm blades. At very low temperatures, meter batteries and other mechanisms may be sluggish, so on a cold day it is a good idea to carry the camera under your coat until you're ready to take a picture. On the beach, protection from salt spray and sand is vital. Accidental immersion in salt water can occur, however; it is best treated by an immediate and thorough rinse in fresh water, slow drying in a slightly warmed environment (like a gas oven with only the pilot on), followed by a trip to the repair shop as soon as possible. Your only consolation will be that you are not the first one to have this happen.

If a camera will not be used for a while, release the shutter, turn off the exposure meter, and store the camera away from excessive heat, humidity, and dust. Operate the shutter occasionally, because it may become balky if not used. For long-term storage, remove batteries, since they can corrode and leak.

Protecting a camera from dust and dirt is the primary purpose of ordinary camera care. Load and unload film or change lenses in a dust-free place if you possibly can. When changing film, blow or brush around the camera's film-winding mechanism and along the film path. This will remove dust as well as tiny bits of film that can break off and work into the camera's mechanisms. Be careful of the shutter curtain when doing this; it is delicate and should be touched only with extreme care. You may want to blow occasional dust off the focusing mirror or screen, but a competent camera technician should do any work beyond this. Never lubricate any part of the camera yourself.

The lens surface must be clean for best performance, but keeping dirt off of it in the first place is much better than too-frequent cleaning, which can damage the delicate lens coating. Particularly avoid touching the lens surface with your fingers, because they can leave oily prints that may corrode the coating. Keep a lens cap on the front of the lens when it is not in use and on the back of the lens as well if the lens is removed from the camera. During use, a lens hood helps protect the lens surface in addition to shielding the lens from stray light.

To clean the lens you will need a soft rubber squeeze bulb, like an ear syringe, a soft brush, lens tissue, and lens cleaning fluid. Avoid cleaning products made for eyeglasses; they are too harsh for lens surfaces. Shirttails, a clean handkerchief, or paper tissues are usable in an emergency, but lens tissue is much better. ▪

Cleaning inside the camera When you blow or dust inside the camera, tip the camera so the dust falls out and isn't pushed farther into the mechanism. Do not touch the delicate shutter curtain unless absolutely necessary.

Cleaning the lens First, blow or brush any visible dust off the lens surface. Holding the lens upside down helps the dust fall off the surface instead of just circulating on it.

Using lens cleaning fluid Dampen a wadded piece of tissue with the fluid and gently wipe the lens in a circular direction. Don't put lens fluid directly on the lens since it can run to the edge and soak into the barrel. Finish with a gentle, circular wipe with a dry tissue.

Vivitar Corp.

Forming an image Although a good lens is essential for making crisp, sharp photographs, you don't actually need one to take pictures. A primitive camera can be constructed from little more than a shoebox with a small pinhole at one end and a piece of film at the other. A pinhole won't do as well as a lens, but it does form an image of objects in front of it.

A simple lens, as in a magnifying glass, will also form an image—one that is brighter and sharper than an image formed by a pinhole. But a simple lens has many optical defects or aberrations that prevent it from forming an image that is sharp and accurate. A modern compound lens eliminates these aberrations by combining several lens elements ground to different thicknesses and curvatures so that in effect they cancel out each other's aberrations.

Lens speed The main function of lenses is to project a sharp image onto the film, but, in addition, lenses vary in design, with different types made to perform some jobs better than others. The two major differences are in speed and focal length. Lens speed is not the same as shutter speed; it is rather the widest aperture to which the lens diaphragm can be opened. A lens that is "faster" than another opens to a wider aperture and admits more light; it can be used in dimmer light or at a faster shutter speed.

Lens focal length Even more important is focal length. One of the advantages of a single-lens-reflex camera is the interchangeability of its lenses; the reason photographers own more than one lens is so they can change lens focal length. More about focal length on the following pages. ▪

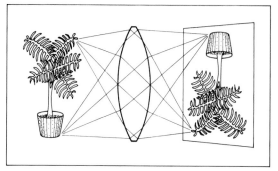

A simple lens forms an image of an object, but because of inherent defects or aberrations in this type of lens, the image is subject to various distortions and is not very sharp.

A modern compound lens combines several lenses ground to different specifications that largely cancel out each other's defects. In recent years lens designers, aided by computers, have produced a great variety of new lenses with improved image sharpness and lens speed.

LENS FOCAL LENGTH: THE BASIC DIFFERENCE BETWEEN LENSES

Photographers generally describe lenses in terms of their focal length; they refer to a normal, long, or short lens, a 100mm lens, a 75–150mm zoom lens, and so on. Focal length affects the image formed on the film in two important and related ways: the amount of the scene shown (the angle of view) and thus the size of objects (their magnification).

How focal length affects an image
The shorter the focal length of a lens, the more of a scene the lens takes in and the smaller it makes each object in the scene appear in the image. You can demonstrate this by looking through a circle formed by your thumb and forefinger. The shorter the distance between your hand (the lens) and your eye (the film), the more of the scene you will see (the greater the angle of view), and since more objects will be shown on the same size negative, the smaller all of them will have to be (the less the magnification). This is similar to the difference between filling a negative with an image of one person's head or with a group of twenty people. In the group portrait, each person's head is smaller.

Interchangeable lenses are convenient. The amount of the scene shown and the size of objects can also be changed by moving the camera closer to or farther from the subject, but the additional option of changing lens focal length gives you much more flexibility and control. Sometimes it is impossible to get closer to your subject—for example, if you are standing on shore photographing a boat on a lake. Sometimes it is difficult to get far enough away, as when you are photographing a large group of people in a small room.

With a single-lens-reflex you can remove one lens and put on another when you want to change focal length. Interchangeable lenses range from super-wide-angle fisheye lenses to extra-long telephotos. A zoom lens is a single lens with adjustable focal lengths. ∎

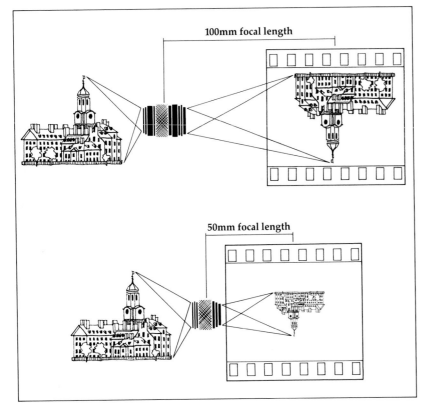

100mm focal length

50mm focal length

Focal length is measured from the optical center of a lens to the image it forms on the film. It is measured when the lens is sharply focused on an object in the far distance (technically known as infinity). Magnification, the size of an object in an image, is one important characteristic that is affected by focal length. As the focal length increases, the size of the object increases. A 100mm lens produces an image twice as large as one produced by a 50mm lens.

24mm

84°

50mm

47°

100mm

24°

200mm

12°

500mm

5°

1000mm
focal length

2.5° angle of view

What happens when you change lens focal length? With a given size of film, the amount of a scene included in the image (angle of view) and the size of objects (magnification) are changed if the focal length of the lens is changed. To make this sequence, the photographer changed only the focal length of the lenses, while the distance from lens to subject remained the same. As the focal length increased, for example, from 24mm to 50mm, the angle of view narrowed and the size of objects increased.

NORMAL FOCAL LENGTH: THE MOST LIKE HUMAN VISION

In photography, as in most things, *normal* implies that something is similar to the way most people do or see things. A lens of normal focal length, as you might expect, produces an image on film that seems normal when compared with human vision. The image includes about the same angle of view as the human eye sees clearly, and the relative size and spacing of near and far objects appear normal. For 35mm cameras, this effect is produced by a lens of about 50mm focal length, and 35mm cameras typically are fitted by manufacturers with lenses of this type. The size of the film used in a particular camera determines what focal length is normal for that camera; cameras that use film sizes larger than 35mm have proportionately longer focal lengths for their normal lenses.

Normal lenses have many advantages. Compared with those of shorter or longer focal length, normal lenses are generally faster: they can be designed with wider maximum apertures to admit the maximum amount of light.

Therefore, they are the most suitable lenses for low light levels, especially where action is involved, as in theater or indoor sports scenes or in low light levels outdoors. They are a good choice if the camera is to be hand held since a wide maximum aperture permits a shutter speed fast enough to eliminate lens movement during exposure. Generally, the normal lens is more compact and lighter in weight, as well as somewhat less expensive, than comparable lenses of longer or shorter focal length.

Normal focal length can vary. The "normal" focal length used by a particular photographer—the focal length lens usually fitted on his or her camera—is a matter of personal preference. Many photographers use a lens with a focal length of 35mm as their normal lens because they like its wider view and greater depth of field. Some use an 85mm lens because they prefer its narrower view, which can concentrate the image on the central objects of interest in the scene. ▪

Walter Palmer

Charles O'Rear

▲

◀ **A lens of normal focal length** produces an image that appears similar to that of normal human vision. The amount of the scene included in the image and the relative size and placement of near and far objects are what you would expect to see if you were standing by the camera. The scene does not appear exaggerated in depth, as it might with a short-focal-length lens, nor do the objects seem compressed and too close together, as sometimes happens with a long-focal-length lens.

LONG FOCAL LENGTH: TELEPHOTO LENSES

A lens of long focal length seems to bring things closer, just as a telescope does. As the focal length gets longer, less of the scene is shown (the angle of view narrows), but what is shown is enlarged (the magnification increases). This is useful when you are so far from the subject that a lens of normal focal length produces an image that is too small. Sometimes you can't get really close—at a sports event, for example; sometimes it is better to stay at a distance, as in nature photography. An intercepted pass, the President descending from Air Force One, and an erupting volcano are all possible subjects for which you might want a long lens.

A long lens has relatively little depth of field. When you use long lenses, you'll also notice that as the focal length increases, depth of field decreases so that less of the scene is in focus at any given f-stop. For example, a 200mm lens at f/8 has less depth of field than a 100mm lens at f/8. Sometimes this is inconvenient—for example, if you want objects in the foreground of a scene as well as those in the background to be sharp. But it can also work to your advantage by permitting you to eliminate unimportant details or a busy background by photographing them out of focus.

A long lens can seem to compress space. Though traffic was heavy in New York on the day this picture was taken, the long-focal-length lens used by the photographer made the scene look even more crowded than it was. When do you get this effect, and why? See pages 34–35 to find out.

Dan McCoy

Fredrik D. Bodin

Portrait with a medium-long lens A medium-long lens of 85–135 mm is particularly useful for portraits because the photographer can be relatively far from the subject and still fill the image frame. Many people feel more at ease when photographed if the camera is not too close, and a moderate distance between camera and subject eliminates the distortion of perspective that occurs when a lens is used very close. A good working distance would be 6–8 ft. (2–2.5 m).

Portrait with shorter lens To get a head-and-shoulders image of the same subject with a lens of normal focal length (50 mm), the photographer had to move in close. Photographing a person from very close makes the size of the features nearest to the camera unnaturally large and sometimes even grotesque. If this same lens were used farther back, the subject's head would be small, perhaps too small to enlarge to the desired size without loss of quality.

A long lens, compared with one of normal focal length, is larger, heavier, and somewhat more expensive. Its largest aperture is relatively small; f/4 or f/5.6 is not uncommon. It must be focused carefully because with its shallow depth of field there will be a distinct difference between objects that are sharply focused and those that are not. A faster shutter speed is needed to hand hold because the enlarged image magnifies even a slight movement of the lens during exposure. These disadvantages increase as the focal length increases, but so do the long lens's unique image-forming characteristics. ▪

SHORT FOCAL LENGTH: WIDE-ANGLE LENSES

Lenses of short focal length are also called wide-angle or wide-field lenses, which describes their most important feature—they view a wider angle of a scene than human vision does. A lens of normal focal length records what you see when you look at a scene with eyes fixed in one position. A wide-angle lens is like sweeping your vision from side to side, from your left shoulder to your right shoulder for the 180° viewing angle of a 7.5 fisheye lens or slightly from side to side for the 63° angle of a lens of 35mm focal length.

A short lens has great depth of field. The shorter the focal length of a lens, the more of a scene that will be sharp (if the f-stop and distance from the subject remain unchanged). A 28mm lens stopped down to f/8 can be sharp from less than 6.5 ft. (2 m) to infinity (as far as the eye or lens can see), which often will eliminate the need for focusing once the lens has been preset for maximum depth of field.

Wide-angle "distortion" A wide-angle lens can seem to distort an image and produce strange perspective effects. Sometimes these effects are actually caused by the lens, as with a fisheye lens (page 29). But, more often, what seems to be distortion in an image made with a wide-angle lens is caused by the photographer shooting very close to the subject, which is easy to do with this type of lens. A 28mm lens, for example, will focus as close as 1 ft. (0.3 m), and shorter lenses even closer. Any object seen from close up appears larger than an object of the same size that is at a distance. While you are at a scene, your brain knows if you are very close to an object and ordinarily you would not even notice any visual exaggeration. In a photograph, however, you notice size comparisons immediately. See photographs at right. ▪

Short lenses are popular with photojournalists, feature photographers, and others who shoot in fast-moving and sometimes crowded situations. For example, many photojournalists use 35mm or 28mm lenses instead of 50mm (normal-focal-length) lenses. These medium-short lenses give a wider angle of view than a 50mm lens, which makes it easier to photograph in close quarters (as in this family dining room). Medium-short lenses also have more depth of field, which can let a photographer focus the lens approximately, instead of having to fine-focus every shot.

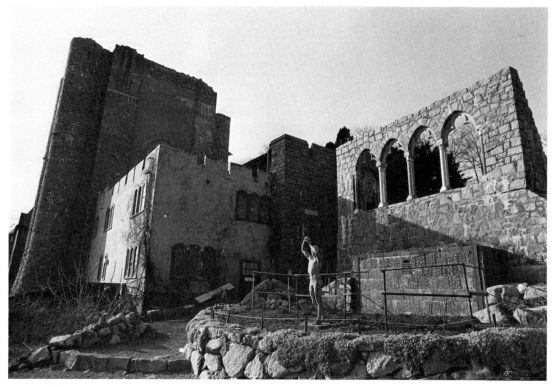

Short lenses show a wide view. Short-focal-length lenses are useful for including a wide view of an area. They have great depth of field so that objects both close to the lens and far from it will be in focus, even at a relatively large aperture.

Fredrik D. Bodin

Objects up close appear larger. A short lens can produce strange perspective effects. Since it can be focused at very close range, it can make objects in the foreground large in relation to those in the background. With the lens close to the statue, it looks larger relative to the buildings behind it than it does in the photograph above.

ZOOM, MACRO, AND FISHEYE LENSES

In addition to the usual range of short-, normal-, and long-focal-length lenses, there are other lenses that can view a scene in a new way or solve certain problems with ease.

Zoom lenses combine a range of focal lengths into one lens (see below). The glass elements of the lens can be moved in relation to each other; thus infinitely variable focal lengths are available within the limits of the zooming range. Using a 50–135mm zoom, for example, is like having a 50mm, 85mm, and 135mm lens instantly available, plus any focal length in between. Though zoom lenses are relatively high-priced and somewhat bulky and heavy, one of them will replace two or more fixed-focal-length lenses. Zoom lenses are best used where light is ample since they have a relatively small maximum aperture. New designs give considerably improved sharpness compared with earlier zoom lenses, which were significantly less sharp than fixed-focal-length lenses.

Macro lenses are used for close-up photography (opposite, top). Their optical design corrects for the focusing faults that can occur at very short focusing distances, but they can also be used at normal distances. Their main disadvantage is relatively small maximum aperture, often about f/3.5 for a 50mm lens. (More about close-up photography in Chapter 5.)

Fisheye lenses have a very wide angle of view—up to 180°—and they exaggerate to an extreme degree differences in size between objects that are close to the camera and those that are farther away (opposite, bottom). They actually distort the image by bending straight lines at the edges of the picture. ▪

A zoom lens gives you a choice of different focal lengths within the same lens. The rectangles overlaid on the picture show some of the ways you could have made this photograph by zooming in to shoot at a long focal length or zooming back to shoot at a shorter one.

Richard Frear

A macro lens enabled the photographer to move in very close to this denizen of the Florida Everglades without having to use supplemental close-up attachments such as extension tubes.

A fisheye lens bent the buildings in this city scene into a round globe shape. Objects at the edge of the fisheye's image circle are distorted more than they are toward the center.

DEPTH OF FIELD: SHARPNESS IN A PHOTOGRAPH

Depth of field Dead sharp from foreground to background, totally out of focus except for a narrow strip, or sharp to any extent in between—it is possible to choose how sharp your image will be. When you focus a camera on an object, the distance between lens and film is adjusted by turning the lens barrel until the object is sharp on the viewing screen. In most cases part of the scene will be acceptably sharp both in front of and behind the most sharply focused plane. Objects will gradually become more and more out of focus the farther they are from the sharply focused area. This depth within which objects appear acceptably sharp in the image—the depth of field—can to a certain extent be increased or decreased.

The depth of field, the area in a scene that is acceptably sharp, extended in the top picture on this page from the flowers in the foreground to the greenhouse windows in the background. For another picture (bottom) the photographer wanted only part of the scene to be sharp. See opposite for ways to control the depth of field in a photograph.

Alan Oransky

Controlling the depth of field When you make a picture you can manipulate three things that affect the depth of field (illustrations opposite). Notice that changing the depth of field may at the same time change the image in other ways.

Aperture size Stopping down the lens to a smaller aperture, for example, from f/2 to f/16, increases the depth of field. As the aperture gets smaller, more of the scene will be sharp in the print.

Focal length Using a shorter-focal-length lens also increases the depth of field at any given f-number. For example, more of a scene will be sharp when photographed with a 50mm lens at f/8 than with a 200mm lens at f/8.

Lens-to-subject distance Moving farther away from the subject increases the depth of field most of all, and simply stepping back with your camera will make more of a scene sharp in the print. This is particularly true if you start out very close to the subject. ▪

The smaller the aperture (with a given lens), the greater the depth of field. Using a smaller aperture for the picture on the right made the image much sharper. With the smaller aperture, the amount of light reaching the film decreased, so a slower shutter speed had to be used to keep the total exposure the same.

The shorter the focal length of the lens, the greater the depth of field. Notice that changing to a shorter focal length for the picture on the right also changed the angle of view (the amount of the scene shown) and the magnification of objects in the scene.

The farther you are from a subject, the greater the depth of field. The photographer stepped back to take the picture on the right. If you focus on an object far enough away, the lens will form a sharp image of all objects from that point out to infinity.

Fredrik D. Bodin

Fredrik D. Bodin

Fredrik D. Bodin

MORE ABOUT DEPTH OF FIELD: HOW TO PREVIEW IT

When photographing a scene, you will often want to know the extent of the depth of field—how much of the scene will be sharp. You may want to be sure that certain objects are sharp. Or you may deliberately want something out of focus, such as a distracting background. To control what is sharp, you need some way of gauging the depth of field.

With zone focusing you can be ready for an action shot by focusing in advance, if you know approximately where the action will take place. Suppose you are on a ski slope and you want to photograph a skier coming down the hill. The nearest point at which you might want to take the picture is 15 ft. (4.5 m) from the action; the farthest is 30 ft. (9 m).

Line up the distance scale so that these two distances are opposite a pair of f-stop indicators on the depth-of-field scale (with the lens shown at right, below the two distances fall opposite the f/16 indicators). Now, if your aperture is set to f/16 or smaller, everything from 15–30 ft. (4.5–9 m) will be within the depth of field and in focus.

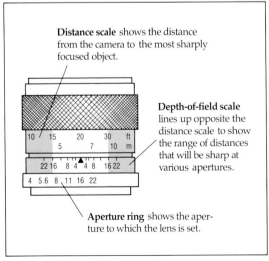

Distance scale shows the distance from the camera to the most sharply focused object.

Depth-of-field scale lines up opposite the distance scale to show the range of distances that will be sharp at various apertures.

Aperture ring shows the aperture to which the lens is set.

Checking the depth of field For viewing, the lens aperture is ordinarily wide open, and the viewing screen shows the scene with the depth of field at its shallowest. When the shutter release is pressed, the lens automatically stops down to the taking aperture and the depth of field increases. Some cameras have a previewing mechanism so that, if you wish, you can stop down the lens to view the scene at the taking aperture and see how much will be sharp.

However, if the lens is set to a very small aperture, the stopped-down image on the screen may be too dark to be seen clearly. If so, the nearest and farthest limits of the depth of field can be read on the depth-of-field scale on the lens barrel (this page, bottom). Manufacturers also prepare printed tables showing the depth of field for different lenses at various focusing distances and f-stops.

Zone focusing for action Knowing the depth of field in advance is useful when you want to preset the lens to be ready for an action shot without last-minute focusing. Zone focusing uses the depth-of-field scale on the lens to set the focus and aperture so that the action will be photographed well within the depth of field (this page, top).

Focusing for the greatest depth of field When you are shooting a scene that includes important objects at a long distance as well as some that are closer, you will want maximum depth of field. Shown opposite is a way of setting the lens to permit as much as possible of the scene to be sharp. ▪

When the lens is focused on infinity (∞ on the lens distance scale), everything at that point or farther away will be sharp: with this lens at f/22 everything will be sharp from 50 ft. (16 m) to infinity (as far as the eye can see). In the picture at left everything is sharp from the bushes in the pasture to the farthest point in the background.

Fredrik D. Bodin

You can increase the depth of field even more if, instead of focusing on infinity, you set the infinity mark (∞) opposite the point on the depth-of-field scale that shows the f-stop you are using. You are now focused on a distance (50 ft., 16 m.) slightly closer than infinity (technically called the hyperfocal distance). Now everything from the plank of the fence in the foreground (25 ft., 8 m) to the far background is within the depth of field and will be sharp in the print.

PERSPECTIVE: HOW A PHOTOGRAPH SHOWS DEPTH

Perspective: the impression of depth Few lenses (except for the fisheye) actually distort reality. The perspective in a photograph—the apparent size and shape of objects and the impression of depth—is what you would see if you were standing at camera position. Why then do some photographs seem to have an exaggerated depth, with the subject appearing stretched and expanded (this page, top), while other photographs seem to show a compressed space, with objects crowded very close together (this page, bottom)? The brain judges depth in a photograph mostly by comparing objects in the foreground with those in the background, and the greater the size differences perceived, the greater the impression of depth. When viewing an actual scene, the brain has other clues to the actual distances, and it disregards any apparent distortion in sizes. But when looking at a photograph, the brain uses relative sizes as the major clue.

How perspective is controlled in a photograph Any lens moved in very close to the foreground of a scene increases the impression of depth by increasing the size of foreground objects relative to objects in the background. As shown opposite, perspective is not affected by changing the focal length of the lens if the camera remains at the same distance. However, it does change if the distance from lens to subject is changed.

Perspective can be exaggerated. Perspective effects are exaggerated when changes occur in both focal length and lens-to-subject distance. A short-focal-length lens used close to the subject increases differences in size because it is much closer to foreground objects than to those in the background. This increases the impression of depth. Distances are magnified and sizes and shapes may be distorted when scenes are photographed in this way.

The opposite effect occurs with a long-focal-length lens used far from the subject. Differences in sizes are decreased because the lens is relatively far from *all* objects. This decreases the apparent depth and sometimes seems to squeeze objects into a smaller space than they could occupy in reality. ▪

Expanded perspective A short-focal-length lens used close to a subject stretches distances because it magnifies objects near the lens in relation to those that are far from the lens.

Compressed perspective A long-focal-length lens used far from a subject compresses space. Size differences and the impression of depth are minimized because the lens is relatively far from both foreground and background.

Fredrik D. Bodin

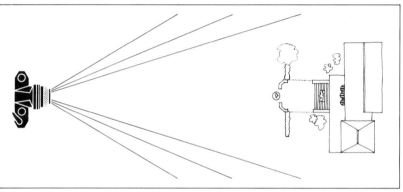

Changing focal length alone does not change perspective—the apparent size or shape of objects or their apparent position in depth. As the focal length was increased for the photographs above, the size of all the objects increased at the same rate. Thus, the impression of depth remained the same.

Lens-to-subject distance controls perspective. Perspective is changed when the distance from the lens to objects in the scene is changed. Here, though the focal length remained the same, the impression of depth increased as the camera was brought closer to the subject.

Alan Oransky

LENS PERFORMANCE: GETTING THE MOST FROM A LENS

Lens motion causes blur. Though some photographers claim to be able to hand hold their cameras steadily at slow shutter speeds—1/15 sec. or even slower—it takes only a slight amount of lens motion during exposure to cause a noticeable blur in an image. If a sharp picture is your aim, using a fast shutter speed or supporting the camera on a tripod is a much safer bet for producing an image that will be sharp when enlarged.

1. To hand hold a camera steadily, keep feet apart and rest the camera lightly against your face. Hold your breath and squeeze the shutter release gently.
2. With the camera in a vertical position, the left hand focuses and holds the camera with the left elbow against the chest. The right arm is raised to release the shutter.

3. In this vertical position, the right hand holds the camera and releases the shutter; the left hand focuses and helps steady the camera.
4. In kneeling position, kneel on one leg and rest your upper arm on the other knee. Leaning against a wall or a steady object will help brace your body.

5. With a long lens on the camera, use one hand to support the weight of the lens. Winding the camera strap around your wrist helps to steady the camera and to prevent dropping it.
6. A tripod and cable release provide the steadiest support and are essential for slow shutter speeds if a sharp image is desired.

Preventing blur due to lens motion
The focal length of the lens you are using determines how fast a shutter speed you need to keep an image acceptably sharp during a hand-held exposure. The longer the focal length, the faster the shutter speed must be, because a long lens magnifies any motion of the lens during the exposure just as it magnifies the size of the objects photographed. As a general rule, the slowest shutter speed that is safe to hand hold can be matched to the focal length of the lens. That is, a 50mm lens should be hand held at a shutter speed of 1/50 sec. or faster, a 100mm lens at 1/100 sec. or faster, and so on. This doesn't mean that the camera can be freely moved during the exposure. At these speeds the camera can be hand held, but with care. At the moment of exposure, hold your breath and squeeze the shutter release smoothly.

A tripod will help you in situations that require a slower shutter speed than is feasible for hand holding, for example, at dusk when the light is dim. A tripod is also useful when you want to compose a picture carefully or do close-up work. It is standard equipment for copy work, such as photographing another photograph or something from a book, because hand holding at even a fast shutter speed will not give the critical sharpness that resolves fine details to the maximum degree possible. A cable release also helps by triggering the shutter without your having to touch the camera directly, so the camera stays absolutely still.

Stray light can cause problems. You can't make an exposure without light, but light can also be the undoing of your picture. The sun, a bright bulb, or other light source within the image can cause ghosting, bright spots in the shape of the lens diaphragm that show in the picture. The spots are caused by stray light bouncing around inside the lens.

Flare, an overall graying of the image, is also caused by stray light. Though the sun itself was not in the picture below left, sunlight struck the lens at an angle. The result was an additional exposure of non-image-forming light that reduced picture contrast.

A lens hood helps. Flare is best controlled by using a lens hood or shade to shield the lens from direct light. Lens hoods come in different sizes and should be matched to the focal length of your lens. Too small a hood can cut into the image and vignette the edges (below, right). Check the viewfinder image carefully for vignetting if you are using a filter plus a lens hood or two filters together. ▪

Fredrik D. Bodin

Fredrik D. Bodin

◄**Light problems** Flare (far left) grays the image when light strikes the front of the lens, even if the light source is not in the picture. Vignetting (left) is the result of using a lens hood that is too small and so cuts into the image area.

◄**Lens hoods** clip or screw onto the front of a lens and are made in different sizes to match different focal lengths.

Chapter 3
· FILM AND EXPOSURE ·

The exposure of film to light is one area in which a little expertise pays off in much better pictures. Exposing the film correctly (that is, setting the shutter speed and aperture so they let in the correct amount of light for a given film and scene) makes the difference between a rich image with realistic tones, dark but detailed shadows, and bright, delicate highlights and a too dark, murky picture or a picture that is barely visible because it is too light.

At the simplest level, you can rely on the chart of exposure recommendations the film manufacturer provides with each roll of film. You can also let an exposure meter or automatic exposure system make decisions for you.

In many cases these standardized procedures will give you a satisfactory exposure. But standard procedures don't work in all situations. If the light source is behind the subject, for example, an average reading will silhouette the subject against the brighter background. This may not be what you want.

You will have more control over your pictures—and be happier with the results—if you know how to interpret the information the meter provides and how to adjust the recommended exposure to give any variation you may choose. You will be able to select what you want to do in a specific situation rather than exposing at random and hoping for the best. ▪

Learning to expose film properly is not hard. To let just the right amount of light into the camera, you need to understand just three things:

1. How the shutter speed and the size of the lens opening (the aperture) work together to control light (pages 10–15).

2. The sensitivity of each kind of film to light—the film's speed (pages 42–43).

3. How to meter the light to measure its brightness and then set the exposure, either automatically or manually (pages 50–55).

FILM CHARACTERISTICS: HOW FILM WORKS

The light sensitivity of film The most basic characteristic of film is that it is light-sensitive; it undergoes a chemical change when exposed to light. Light is energy, a visible form of the wavelike energy that extends in a continuum from radio waves through visible light to gamma rays. These forms of energy differ only in their wavelengths, the distance from the crest of one wave to the crest of the next. The visible part of this spectrum, the light that we see, ranges between 400 and 700 nanometers, or billionths of a meter.

Not all films respond the same way to light. Silver halides, the light-sensitive part of film, respond primarily to blue and ultraviolet wavelengths, but dyes can be incorporated in the emulsion to increase their range of sensitivity. General-purpose black-and-white and color films are panchromatic, or pan; they are designed to be sensitive to most wavelengths of the visible spectrum so that the image they record is similar to that perceived by the human eye. Some special-purpose films are designed to be sensitive to other parts of the spectrum. Orthochromatic (or ortho) black-and-white films are sensitive primarily to blue and green wavelengths. Infrared films are sensitive to infrared wavelengths that are invisible to the eye (see page 46). Since some films are designed to perform certain jobs better than others, it is useful to be aware of their characteristics. ▪

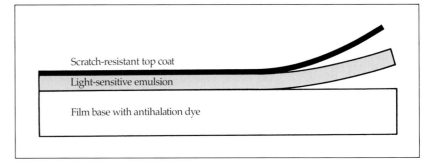

Film cross section
Film is made up of layers of different materials. On top is a tough coating that helps protect the film from scratches during ordinary handling. Next is a layer of gelatin emulsion that contains the light-sensitive part of the film, silver halide crystals. (Color film has several layers of halides, each sensitive to a different part of the spectrum.) An adhesive bonds the emulsion to the base, a flexible support of either cellulose acetate or polyester. To prevent light rays from bouncing back through the film to add unwanted exposure to the emulsion, an antihalation dye that absorbs light is added to the film base.

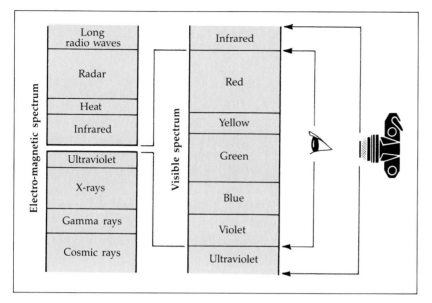

Light When certain wavelengths of energy strike the human eye, they are perceived as light. Film is manufactured so that it too is sensitive to this part of the electromagnetic energy spectrum. In addition, film is sensitive and responds to certain wavelengths that the eye cannot see, such as ultraviolet and infrared light.

Film terms

Color sensitivity The parts of the visible spectrum to which a film responds. See above.

Film speed The overall sensitivity of a film to light as compared with other films. See next page.

Latitude The degree to which film can be overexposed or underexposed and still produce an acceptable print or slide.

Grain The granularity or speckled effect produced by tiny specks of silver in the emulsion clumping together. See next page.

Contrast The range of tones from dark to light that a film produces. Films of normal contrast show blacks, whites, and a wide range of tones in between. High-contrast black-and-white films record all the tones in a scene as either black or white or something close to these extremes.

Emulsion The light-sensitive coating applied to photographic films and papers. It consists of silver halide crystals of silver chloride, silver bromide, and silver iodide, plus other chemicals, suspended in gelatin. The ability of silver halides to darken on exposure to light makes photography possible.

Base The backing of film or paper on which emulsion is coated.

Negative An image, usually on film, with tones that are the opposite of those in the original scene; light areas in the original are dark in the negative, dark areas are light.

Positive An image on paper or film with tones that are the same as those in the original scene.

Transparency Usually, a positive color image on film. A slide is a transparency mounted in a small frame of cardboard or other material so it can be inserted in a projector or viewer.

Reversal processing The procedure by which a positive image is made directly from a scene or from another positive; making a color slide directly from film exposed in the camera is an example.

FILM SPEED AND GRAIN: THE TWO GO TOGETHER

Film speed ratings How sensitive a film is to light, that is, how much it darkens when exposed to a given quantity of light, is indicated by its film speed number (in English-speaking countries, an ISO or ASA rating). The more sensitive—or faster—the film, the higher its number in the rating system. (See box opposite: Film speed ratings.)

A high film speed is often useful: the faster the film, the less exposure it needs to produce an image, and so fast films are often used for photographing in dim light. But along with fast film speed go some other characteristics: an increase in grain and decrease in contrast and often in sharpness. As the illustrations on this page show, the most detailed image was produced by the slow, ASA 32 film. The very fast ASA 2475 film, by comparison, gave a mottled, grainy effect and recorded less detail.

Graininess occurs when the bits of silver that form the image clump together. It is more likely to occur with fast films, which have large silver halide crystals, than it is with slower films having smaller crystals. The effect is more noticeable in big enlargements or if the film is not processed at consistent temperatures, if it is overexposed, or if it is "pushed" to increase its film speed by special development.

What film speed should you use? Theoretically, for maximum sharpness you should choose the slowest film usable in a given situation. For practical purposes, however, many photographers use a medium-fast (ASA 100–200) film in most situations and switch to a slow film only when extremely fine detail is of special importance. ▪

ASA 32 **ASA 400** **ASA 2475**

Film speed and grain Generally speaking, the slower the film (the lower the ASA, DIN, or ISO number), the finer the grain structure of the film and the more detailed the image the film records. Compare these extreme enlargements. Film speed also affects the color qualities of color materials like slide films.

Alan Oransky

Slower film speed ⟵— Less grain
— More detail
— More contrast

Film speed ratings

Film speeds are given in one of three rating systems: ASA, DIN, or ISO. Film manufacturers are now standardizing film speed listings, using the ISO system, which may in time simplify things. Don't be overly concerned about the numerical soup; the first thing to remember is simply that the higher the number in a given rating system, the faster the film, that is, the less light it will need for a correct exposure.

An ASA (American Standards Association) rating is found on films sold in English-speaking countries. Each time the ASA number doubles, the film speed doubles. ASA 200 is twice as fast as ASA 100, half as fast as ASA 400.

A DIN (Deutsche Industrie Norm) rating is common in European countries. Each time the rating increases by 3, the film speed doubles. DIN 24 (equivalent to ASA 200) is twice as fast as DIN 21, half as fast as DIN 27.

The ISO (International Standards Association) system is becoming the universal rating system for film speed listings, but ISO-rated films may still vary somewhat in the way they are listed. A film with a speed equivalent to ASA 200 (DIN 24) may be listed as ISO 200/24 (combining the ASA and DIN numbers), ISO/ASA 200, or simply ISO 200.

Larry Rana

A fast film, ASA 400, let the photographer use a shutter speed of 1/500 sec., fast enough to guarantee that action would be sharp in the picture and fast enough to let him shoot freely, hand holding the camera, without fear that camera motion would blur the picture overall. A fast film is particularly important indoors or when light is dim, but was useful even in this scene outdoors.

A slow film, ASA 32, ▶ recorded fine detail and texture in this forest scene. The image would be crisp and detailed even if enlarged to a much bigger size than shown here.

Daniel O. Todd

BUYING AND USING FILM

Buying film Whatever kind of film you buy, check the expiration date printed on the film package before you make your purchase. The film will still be usable beyond that date but it will steadily deteriorate.

Storing film Heat accelerates the deterioration of film, so avoid storing it in warm places like the inside of a glove compartment on a hot day or the top of a radiator on a cold one. Room temperature is fine for short-term storage, but for longer storage a refrigerator or freezer is better. Be sure that the film to be chilled is in a moisture-proof wrapping, and when you remove the film from refrigeration, avoid condensation of moisture on the film surface by letting it come to room temperature before opening.

Airport security X-ray devices are supposed to be safe for film. However, they can cause fogging of either unexposed or exposed but undeveloped film if the machines are not adjusted correctly or if the same film is subjected to repeated doses, for example, on a trip that involves several flights. Lead-lined film bags are available that give protection from X-rays. Or you can simply ask to have film (and camera, if it is loaded) inspected by hand to reduce the possibility of X-ray damage.

Loading Light exposes film, and you want only the light that comes through the lens to strike the film. So, load and unload your camera away from strong light to avoid the possibility of stray light leaking into film cassettes and causing streaks of unwanted exposure. Outdoors, at least block direct sun by shading the camera with your body when loading it. ▪

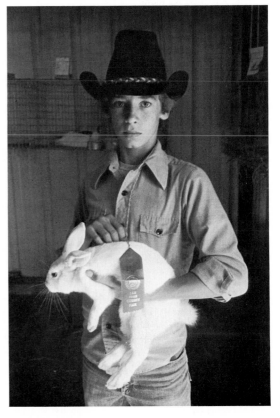

John Running

A fast film, such as one rated at ASA 400 or 1000, is good not only for action shots but for any situation in which the light is relatively dim and you want to work with a fast shutter speed or a small aperture.

B. W. Muir

A medium-speed film, ASA 125, was chosen for this photograph of a forest road. The fine grain and excellent sharpness of the film recorded every detail of the delicate shading on the tree trunks and intricate pattern of leaves.

SPECIAL-PURPOSE FILMS: HIGH-CONTRAST AND INFRARED

Most films are designed to "see" as the human eye does and to respond to light in ways that appear realistic. But some films depart from the reality that we know.

High-contrast black-and-white film does not record a continuous range of tones from black through many shades of gray to white; instead it translates each tone in a scene into either black or white (see illustration below). Some 35mm materials are specially made for high-contrast photography. Some continuous-tone films (like Panatomic X) can also be specially processed for high contrast.

Infrared black-and-white film is sensitized to wavelengths that are invisible to the human eye, the infrared waves that lie between visible red light and wavelengths that produce heat. Since the film responds to light that is not visible to the eye, it can be used to photograph in the dark. The sun is a strong source of infrared radiation, and tungsten filament lamps, flash bulbs, and electronic flash can also be used. Unusual and strangely beautiful images are possible because many materials reflect and absorb infrared radiation differently from visible light (see opposite). Grass, leaves, and other vegetation reflect infrared wavelengths very strongly and thus appear very bright, even white. Clouds too are highly reflective of infrared wavelengths, but since the blue sky does not reflect them, it appears dark, even black, in a print.

Because the wavelengths are invisible, you cannot fully visualize in advance just what the print will look like—sometimes a frustration, but sometimes an unexpected pleasure. The correct exposure is also something of a guess; most meters do not measure infrared light accurately. (See box opposite: Using infrared film.) Infrared color film is also available. ▪

High-contrast film changes the many shades of gray in an ordinary scene into a graphic abstraction of blacks and whites.

Stanley Rowin

Peter Laytin

Infrared film records leaves and grass as very light. The result can be a strangely dreamlike landscape.

Using infrared film

Storage and loading Infrared film can be fogged by exposure to heat or even slight exposure to infrared radiation. Do not buy infrared film that is not refrigerated, and once you have it, store it under refrigeration when possible. Load and unload the camera in total darkness, either in a darkroom or with the camera in a changing bag.

Focusing Most lenses focus infrared wavelengths slightly differently from the way they focus visible light. With black-and-white infrared film, after focusing as usual, rack the lens forward very slightly as if you were focusing on an object closer to you. Some lenses have a red indexing mark on the lens barrel to show the adjustment needed. The difference is very slight, so unless depth of field is very shallow (as when you are photographing close up), you can usually make do without any correction. No correction is needed for infrared color film.

Filtration See manufacturer's instructions. Kodak recommends a No. 25 red filter for general use with black-and-white infrared film to enhance the infrared effect by absorbing the blue light to which the film is also sensitive. Kodak recommends a No. 12 minus-blue filter for general use with color infrared film.

Exposure A general-purpose exposure meter, whether built into a camera or hand-held, cannot reliably measure infrared radiation. Kodak recommends the following manually set trial exposures for its films. High-Speed Infrared black-and-white film used with No. 25 filter: distant scenes—1/125 sec. at f/11; nearby scenes—1/30 sec. at f/11. Ektachrome Infrared color film with a No. 12 filter: 1/125 sec. at f/16. After making the trial exposure, make additional exposures of 1/2 stop and 1 stop more and 1/2 stop and 1 stop less (see Bracketing, page 49).

NORMAL, UNDER-, AND OVEREXPOSURE

A negative is the first image that is produced when film is exposed to light. A negative is the reverse of the original scene: the brightest areas in the scene are the darkest in the negative. How does this happen? When light strikes film, the energy of the light activates light-sensitive silver halide crystals in the film emulsion. The energy rearranges the structure of the crystals so that during development they convert to particles of dark metallic silver.

The more light that strikes a particular area, the more the light-sensitive crystals are activated, and the darker that part of the negative will be. As a result, a white canoe, for example, will be very dark in the negative. If film is exposed to light long enough, it darkens simply by the action of light, but ordinarily it is exposed only long enough to produce a latent or invisible image that is then made visible by chemical development.

To get a positive print from the negative, the negative is printed, usually by shining light through it, on a piece of light-sensitive paper. Where the original scene was bright (the white canoes), the negative is very dark and dense with many particles of silver. Dense areas in the negative block light from the positive; few particles of silver form there, and the areas are bright in the final image.

The opposite happens with dark areas like the darker parts of the water in the original scene: dark areas reflect little light, so only a little silver (or sometimes, none) is produced in the negative. When the positive is made, these thin or clear areas in the negative pass much light to the positive and form dark deposits of silver corresponding to the dark areas in the original scene. When a positive transparency like a color slide is made, the negative is chemically processed into a positive.

Exposure determines the darkness of the image. The exposure you give a negative (the combination of f-stop and shutter speed) determines how much light reaches the film and how dark the negative will be: the more light, the darker the negative, and, in general, the lighter the final image. The correct exposure for a given situation depends on how you want the photograph to look.

Film and paper have exposure latitude, that is, a good print can often be made from a less-than-perfect negative. Color slides have the least latitude: for best results they should not be overexposed or underexposed more than ½ stop (1 stop is acceptable for some scenes). See page 63 for more about exposing color film. Black-and-white or color prints can be made from negatives that vary somewhat more: from about 1 stop underexposure to 2 stops overexposure is usually acceptable.

But with too much variation from the correct exposure, prints and slides begin to look bad. Too much light overexposes the negative; it will be much too dense with silver to pass enough light to the final print, which in turn will be too pale (illustrations, opposite bottom). Conversely, too little exposure produces a negative that is too thin, resulting in a print that is much too dark (illustrations, opposite top).

Underexposed negative

Dark positive

Normal negative

Normal positive

Overexposed negative

Light positive

B. W. Muir

Bracketing helps if you are not sure about the exposure. To bracket, you take several photographs of the same scene at different exposure settings. First make an exposure with the aperture and shutter speed set by the automatic system or manually set at the combination you think is the right one. Then make a second shot with 1 stop more exposure, and a third shot with 1 stop less exposure. This is easy to do if you are setting the exposure manually: for 1 stop more exposure, either set the shutter to the next slower speed or the aperture to the next larger opening (the next smaller f-number); for 1 stop less exposure, either set the shutter to the next faster speed or the aperture to the next smaller opening (the next larger

f-number). Usually, one of the three shots will be about right.

How do you bracket with automatic exposure? That depends on your camera. Some models have an exposure compensation dial with which you can set in a fixed amount of exposure change. Other cameras have a back-light button, which when depressed gives an additional 1 or 1½ stops of exposure. Even if your camera has neither of these features and only functions automatically, so you cannot set the exposure manually, you can still bracket by adjusting the film speed dial: for 1 stop additional exposure, divide the film speed in half and reset the film speed dial accordingly; for 1 stop less exposure, multiply the film speed by 2 and reset the dial. ▪

EXPOSURE METERS: WHAT DIFFERENT TYPES DO

Exposure meters vary in design but they all perform the same basic function. They measure the brightness of light, then, for a given film speed, they calculate f-stop and shutter speed combinations that will produce a properly exposed negative.

Meters built into cameras The light-sensitive part of a camera meter is a photoelectric cell. When the metering system is turned on and the lens of the camera pointed at a subject, the cell measures the brightness of that subject. To use that reading to expose the picture with automatic exposure operation, you set either the aperture or the shutter speed and the camera adjusts the other to let in the correct amount of light. Some cameras may set both shutter speed and aperture. With manual exposure operation, you adjust the aperture and shutter speed based on the viewfinder readout.

Hand-held meters When the cell of a hand-held meter (one that is not built into a camera) is exposed to light it moves a needle across a scale of numbers or activates a digital display. The greater the amount of light, the higher the reading. When the arrow on the calculator dial is set opposite the same number that appears on the needle scale, a series of recommended f-stop and shutter speed combinations are lined up. See illustration below.

Meter batteries Some hand-held meters and all meters built into cameras are powered by small batteries. It is important to check the batteries regularly (see manufacturer's instructions for how to do this). An exhausted battery will cause the meter to give the wrong reading or to cease functioning altogether. ▪

M. Woodbridge Williams

A through-the-lens (TTL) meter, built into the camera, is a key feature of SLR cameras. The viewfinder shows the area that the meter is reading. A TTL meter may be coupled to the camera to set the exposure automatically or it may simply indicate the correct exposure to set.

A hand-held meter is separate from the camera. After measuring the brightness of a subject, the meter's calculator dial or other readout shows recommended f-stop and shutter speed combinations for correct exposure.

Reflected-light meter

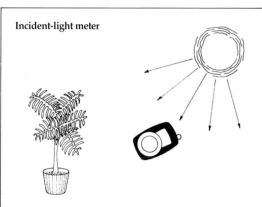

Incident-light meter

◀**A reflected-light meter** measures the amount of light reflected from an object. To make a reading, point the meter at the entire scene or at a specific part of it. Most hand-held meters and all of those built into cameras are reflected-light meters.

◀**An incident-light meter** measures the amount of light falling on an object. The meter's light-sensitive cell is pointed at the camera to measure the amount of light falling on the subject as seen from camera position.

Averaging meter

Center-weighted meter

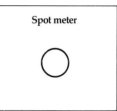

Spot meter

How much of a scene does a reflected-light meter measure? An averaging or overall meter reads most of the image area and computes an exposure that is the average of all the brightnesses in the scene. Center-weighted meters overlap their readings to concentrate on the central area of an image, which is usually the important one to meter. A spot meter reads only a small part of the image. Very accurate exposures can be calculated with a spot meter, but it is important to select with care the area to be read.

Aperture-priority exposure The photographer chooses the aperture, and the camera mechanism adjusts the shutter speed.

Aperture-priority automatic exposure

You set aperture	f/2	f/2.8	f/4	f/5.6	f/8
Shutter speed then adjusts	1/250 sec.	1/125	1/60	1/30	1/15

Cameras with automatic exposure have shutter speed and aperture controls connected to the meter.

Shutter-priority exposure The photographer sets the shutter speed, and the camera mechanism changes the aperture until the correct exposure is set.

Shutter-priority automatic exposure

You set shutter speed	1/250 sec.	1/125	1/60	1/30	1/15
Aperture then adjusts	f/2	f/2.8	f/4	f/5.6	f/8

Programmed exposure The camera sets both shutter speed and aperture.

Programmed automatic exposure

Camera sets shutter speed	1/250 sec.	1/125	1/60	1/30	1/15
Camera sets aperture	f/2	f/2.8	f/4	f/5.6	f/8

MAKING AN EXPOSURE
OF AN AVERAGE SCENE

A single-lens-reflex camera with a built-in meter, and especially a camera with automatic exposure control, makes photography enjoyable and easy. With automatic operation, you simply point the camera at your subject, focus, and shoot. In most cases, the meter and its accompanying automatic circuitry let just the right amount of light in to expose the scene correctly.

A reflected-light meter averages the light entering its angle of view. These meters, whether built into the camera or hand held, are calibrated on the assumption that in an average scene all the tones—dark, medium, and light—will add up to an average medium gray. So the meter and its accompanying circuitry sets, or recommends, an exposure that will record all of the light it is reading as medium gray in the photograph.

This works well if you are photographing an "average" scene, one that has an average distribution of light and dark areas, and if the scene is evenly illuminated as viewed from camera position, that is, when the light is coming more or less from behind you or when the light is evenly diffused over the entire scene (see illustrations this page). The illustrations on the facing page show you how to meter this type of average or low-contrast scene.

A meter can be fooled, however, if your subject is surrounded by a much lighter area such as a bright sky or by a much darker area such as a large dark shadow. See pages 54–55 for what to do in such cases. ▪

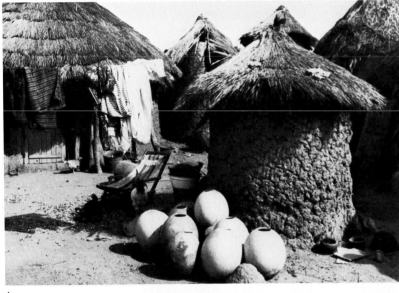

A. Defever

▲
An overall meter reading works well when a directly lit scene is evenly illuminated as seen from camera position. When light is shining directly on a subject, even illumination occurs when the main source of light—here, the sun—is more or less behind you as you face the subject. Shadows are dark but do not obscure important parts of the scene.

◄**A scene in diffused light also photographs well with an overall reading,** for example, outdoors in the shade or on an overcast day or indoors when the light is coming from several light sources. Diffused light is indirect and soft. Shadows are not as dark as they would be in direct light, so all parts of the scene are clearly visible.

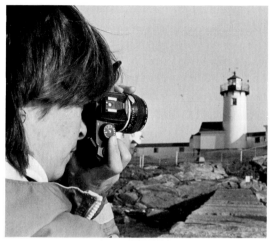

Using a meter built into a camera

1. Set the film speed into the camera.

2. Select the exposure mode: automatic (aperture-priority, shutter-priority, or programmed, if you have a choice) or manual.

3. As you look through the viewfinder at the subject, activate the meter to read the brightness of the scene.

4a. In aperture-priority mode, select an aperture that gives the desired depth of field. The camera will select a shutter speed; make sure that it is fast enough to prevent blurring of the image caused by camera or subject motion.

4b. In shutter-priority mode, select a shutter speed fast enough to prevent blur. The camera will select an aperture; make sure

that it gives the desired depth of field.

4c. In programmed mode, the camera will select both aperture and shutter speed for you.

4d. In manual mode, you set both aperture and shutter speed based on the readout shown in the camera's viewfinder.

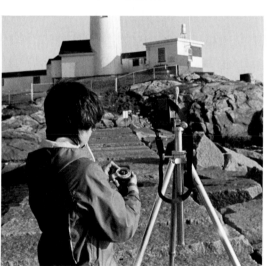

Calculating exposure with a hand-held, reflected-light meter

1. Set the film speed into the meter.

2. Point the meter's photoelectric cell at the subject at the same angle seen by the camera. Activate the meter to measure

the brightness of the light reflected by the subject.

3. Line up the number registered by the indicator needle with the arrow on the meter's calculator dial.

4. Choose one of the combinations of f-stops and shutter

speeds shown on the calculator dial and set the camera accordingly. Any combination shown on the dial lets the same quantity of light into the camera and produces the same exposure.

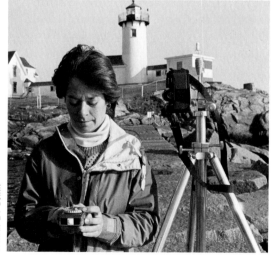

Fredrik D. Bodin

Calculating exposure with an incident-light meter

1. Set the film speed into the meter.

2. Point the meter's photoelectric cell away from the subject—toward the camera lens. Activate the meter to measure the brightness of the light fall-

ing on the subject. (Make sure that the same light that is falling on the subject is falling on the meter. For example, take care not to shade the meter if the subject is brightly lit.)

Proceed as in steps 3 and 4 for reflected-light meter.

EXPOSING SCENES WITH HIGH CONTRAST

"It came out too dark." Sometimes even experienced photographers complain that they metered a scene carefully but the picture still wasn't properly exposed. All an exposure meter or an automatic exposure system can do is measure light. It can't think or reason, so it doesn't know what part of a scene you are interested in or whether a particular object is supposed to be light or dark. You have to think for the meter and sometimes change the exposure it recommends, especially with a scene of high contrast, in which the light areas are much brighter than the dark areas.

What types of scenes cause exposure problems? The most common is a subject against a much brighter background, such as a sunny sky (see illustration below). Because the meter averages all the tonal values—light, medium and dark—in the scene, it assumes that the entire scene is very bright. It consequently sets an exposure that lets in less light, which makes the entire picture darker and your main subject too dark. Less common, but occasionally encountered, is a subject against a very large, much darker background. The meter assumes that the entire scene is very dark, so it lets in more light, which makes the main subject too light.

To expose a contrasty scene correctly you will need to measure the light level for the most important part of the picture. There are several ways to do this. First try to meter just the main subject. If you are photographing a person or some other subject against a much darker or lighter background, move in close enough so that you exclude the background from the reading—though not so close that you meter your own shadow. If your main subject is a landscape or other scene that includes a very bright sky, tilt the camera or meter down slightly so you exclude most of the sky from the reading.

A substitution reading is possible if you can't move in close enough to the important part of a contrasty scene. Look for an object of about the same tone in a similar light that you can read instead. For very exact exposures, professional photographers may meter

Fredrik D. Bodin

An underexposed (too dark) photograph can result when the light is coming from behind the subject or when the subject is against a very bright background such as the sky. The problem is that a meter averages all the tonal values that strike its light-sensitive cell. Here the photographer pointed the meter so it included the much brighter tone of the sky as well as the person.

▲ **A better exposure for contrasty scenes** results from moving up close to meter only the main subject, as shown above. This way, you take your meter reading from the most important part of the scene.

the light reflected from a gray card, a card of standard middle gray of 18 percent reflectance (meters are designed to calculate exposures for ideal subjects of 18 percent reflectance). You can also meter the light reflected by the palm of your hand (see opposite).

How do you set your camera once you have metered a high-contrast scene? If your camera has a manual exposure mode, just set the shutter speed and aperture to expose the main subject correctly, using the settings from a reading made up close or from a substitution reading. In automatic operation, you will need to override the automatic circuitry to change the exposure. Don't be afraid to do this; only you know the picture you want. All cameras have some means of adjusting the exposure (see page 56). ∎

Fredrik D. Bodin

A substitution reading, such as one taken from the palm of your hand, will give you an accurate reading if you can't get close enough to a subject. Try the exposure recommended by the meter if you have very dark skin, but give one stop more exposure if you have light skin, as here.

Fredrik D. Bodin

Move in close to meter a high-contrast scene, where the important part of the picture is either much lighter or much darker than other parts of the image.

With a built-in meter, move in (without blocking the light) until the important area just fills the viewfinder. Set the shutter speed and aperture and move back to your original position to take the picture.

With a hand-held, reflected-light meter, move in close enough to read the subject but not so close as to block the light. A spot meter, which reads light from a very narrow angle of view, is particularly useful for metering high-contrast scenes.

CONTROLLING EXPOSURE

All SLR cameras with automatic exposure have some means of overriding the automatic system when you want to increase the exposure to lighten a picture or decrease the exposure to darken it. The change in exposure is measured in "stops." Each aperture setting is one stop from the next setting. Shutter speeds are also described as being one stop apart; each setting is one stop from the next.

Memory lock   An exposure memory switch temporarily locks in an exposure, so you can move up close to take a reading of a particular area, lock in the desired setting, step back, and then photograph the entire scene.

Exposure compensation dial   Moving the dial to +1 or +2 increases the exposure and lightens the picture. Moving the dial to –1 or –2 decreases the exposure and darkens the picture.

Backlight button   If a camera does not have an exposure compensation dial, it may have a backlight button. Depressing the button adds a fixed amount of exposure, 1½ stops, and lightens the picture. It cannot be used to decrease exposure.

Film speed dial   You can increase or decrease exposure by changing the film speed dial. The camera then responds as if the film is slower or faster than it really is. With ASA- or ISO-rated film, doubling the film speed (for example, from ASA 100 to ASA 200) darkens the picture by decreasing the exposure one stop. Halving the film speed (for example, from ASA 400 to ASA 200) lightens the picture by increasing the exposure one stop.

Manual mode   In manual mode, you adjust the shutter speed and aperture yourself. Exposure can be increased to lighten the picture or decreased to darken it, as you wish.

One or more features for controlling exposure are found on all single-lens-reflex cameras.

You can use manual mode to set the shutter speed and aperture for photographs at night, like this bonfire scene. More about exposures for unusual lighting situations on the following page.

EXPOSURES IN HARD-TO-METER SITUATIONS

What do you do when you want to make a photograph but can't make a meter reading—photographing fireworks, for instance, or a city skyline at night? Guessing and making a couple of experimental tries is better than nothing, and you might get an image you'll like very much. If you keep a record of the scene and your exposures, you will at least have an idea about how to expose a similar scene.

Bracketing is a good idea: make at least three shots—one at the suggested exposure, a second with 1 or 1½ stops more exposure, and a third with 1 or 1½ stops less exposure. Not only will you probably make one exposure that is acceptable, but each different exposure may be best for a different part of the scene. For instance, at night on downtown city streets a longer exposure may show people best while a shorter exposure will be good for brightly lit shop windows.

In hard-to-meter situations, Kodak suggests the manually set exposures at right for films rated at ASA 400. Give twice as much exposure (1 stop more) for films rated at ASA 125 to ASA 200. Give half as much exposure (1 stop less) for films rated at ASA 1000.

For color pictures of scenes marked with * use a tungsten-balanced film for the most natural color.

You can also use daylight-balanced color film, but your pictures will look yellow-red. For color pictures of scenes marked with † use daylight film. You can also use tungsten film with an 85B (amber) filter over your camera lens; if you do this, give 1 stop more exposure than that indicated in the table. (More about film color balance on pages 64–65.)

	With ASA 400 film
*Home interiors at night—areas with average light	1/30 sec. f/2
*Candlelit close-ups	1/15 sec. f/2
Indoor and outdoor holiday lighting at night, Christmas trees	1/15 sec. f/2
Brightly lit downtown streets	1/60 sec. f/2.8
Brightly lit nightclub or theater districts, e.g., Las Vegas	1/60 sec. f/4
Neon signs and other lit signs	1/125 sec. f/4
Store windows	1/60 sec. f/4
Subjects lit by streetlights	1/15 sec. f/2
Floodlit buildings, fountains	1/15 sec. f/2
Skyline—distant view of lit buildings at night	1 sec. f/2.8
Skyline—10 minutes after sunset	1/60 sec. f/5.6
Fairs, amusements parks	1/30 sec. f/2.8
Amusement park rides—light patterns	1 sec. f/16
Fireworks—displays on ground	1/60 sec. f/4
Fireworks—aerial displays (Keep shutter open for several bursts.)	f/16
Lightning (Keep shutter open for one or two streaks.)	f/11
Burning buildings, campfires, bonfires	1/60 sec. f/4
Subjects by campfires, bonfires	1/30 sec. f/2
*Night football, baseball, racetracks	1/125 sec. f/2.8
Niagara Falls—white lights Light-colored lights Dark-colored lights	4 sec. f/5.6 8 sec. f/5.6 15 sec. f/5.6
Moonlit—landscapes Snow scenes	8 sec. f/2 4 sec. f/2
*Basketball, hockey, bowling	1/125 sec. f/2
*Boxing, wrestling	1/250 sec. f/2
*Stage shows—average	1/60 sec. f/2.8
*Circuses—floodlit acts	1/60 sec. f/2.8
*Ice shows—floodlit acts	1/125 sec. f/2.8
†Interiors with bright fluorescent light	1/60 sec. f/4
*School—stage and auditorium	1/30 sec. f/2
*Hospital nurseries	1/60 sec. f/2.8
*Church interiors—tungsten light	1/30 sec. f/2

© Eastman Kodak Company, 1978

Bill Strode

Very long exposures may turn out too dark even if you think the exposure was calculated correctly. The problem here is that a very long exposure at a very low light level does not affect the film as strongly as you would expect it to (technically this is called the reciprocity effect). For exposures of 1 second or longer, increase the total exposure by ½ to 1 stop; for exposures of 10 seconds or longer, increase 1 to 2 stops; for exposures of 100 seconds or longer, increase 2 to 3 stops. See instructions packed with film for more detailed information. ▪

What exposure would you use with ASA 400 film for this shot at dusk of the riverboat "Belle of Louisville"? If the chart at left doesn't have exactly the situation you are photographing, look for a related one. As a start for an exposure for this scene you might try the one recommended for "Skyline—10 minutes after sunset." Then bracket additional exposures.

Chapter 4
· COLOR ·

Why a separate chapter on color? The basic camera-handling techniques are the same as for black and white, and you can load a roll of color film, shoot, and probably get pretty good pictures. But you will get more consistent results and be happier with what you get if you know a little about how color film reacts to light. This chapter describes what to expect from color film and how to use it to make better pictures.

Color slides and prints are appealing because color makes a picture seem more realistic than the same scene rendered in black and white. Black-and-white film records the shapes of things and tones from light to dark, but the black-and-white image is still very much an abstraction. An image in color is more like the real one. It is more apt to remind you of exactly how the scene looked when you took the picture and to make viewers who weren't there feel that they are really seeing the scene too.

Color pictures can also be deliberately *un*realistic. A purple sky, a green horse, color streaks, and other manipulations are possible with color materials and may be just what you want on occasion.

Where does color come from? Light from the sun appears to have no tint or color of its own; it is "white" light. But it actually contains all colors, and if you project it through a prism it will separate into a band of colors like a rainbow. A colored object—a leaf, for example—has color because when light strikes it, the leaf reflects the greenish components or wavelengths of the light while absorbing other colors. The eye is sensitive to these reflected wavelengths and sees them as green. Dyes, in paint or color prints, act just as the leaf does in selectively absorbing and reflecting certain wavelengths of light and so producing color. ▪

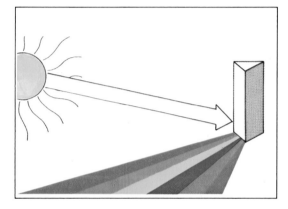

"White" light, such as that from the sun, contains all the colors of the spectrum. Pass light through a prism and it will break into a rainbow of colors.

A lily appears white because it reflects all the wavelengths of light that strike it. When these wavelengths reach the eye, the color white is perceived.

A leaf appears green because when light strikes it, the leaf absorbs all but the wavelengths that create the visual sensation of green.

COLOR FILM CHARACTERISTICS

What can you get in color films?
There are many brands and types of color film on the market. They belong basically to two main categories: negative films and reversal films. A negative film (such as Kodacolor or Agfacolor) produces a negative in which the tones and colors are the opposite of those in the original scene. The negative is then printed on paper or film to make a positive image. A reversal film (such as Kodachrome or Fujichrome) is given special reversal processing to produce a positive transparency or slide.

Color films come in a range of film speeds, from slow (ASA 25) to fast (ASA 1000). Just as with black-and-white films, more film speed brings some increase in grain and decrease in sharpness. Film speed also affects the color rendition of the film, with faster films generally producing less intense colors (less saturation) than slower films. Different films are also made to be used with specific light sources such as sunlight or tungsten light (see pages 64–65).

Negative color film is first processed for a negative image and then the negative is printed to make a positive image. Reversal color film produces the familiar transparency or slide that is viewed by projection; it is a positive color image on the film exposed in the camera. A slide can also be printed on paper, to make another positive image.

Color reversal films vary from brand to brand, and slides of identical film speed from different manufacturers will show variations in color balance, color saturation, grain, and other characteristics. Personal taste is important here, and it is useful to expose the same scene on different types of film and compare the processed slides to choose the film you prefer for future use. Color negative films also vary from brand to brand, but less noticeably than reversal films.

Color film consists of three light-sensitive layers, each of which responds to about one-third of the colors in the light spectrum. Each layer is matched to a primary color dye that is built into the emulsion or added during processing, and every color in the spectrum can be produced by mixing varying proportions of these color primaries.

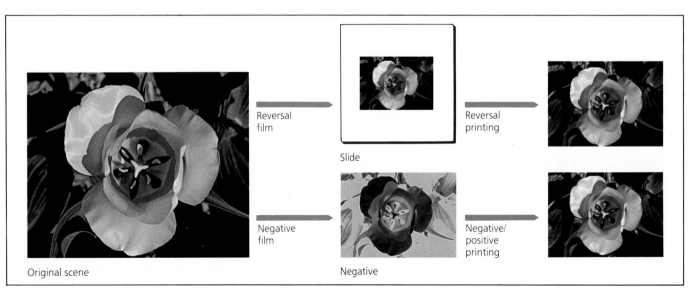

Original scene

Reversal film → Slide → Reversal printing

Negative film → Negative → Negative/positive printing

Correct exposure is essential for slides. If you want slides with clear, brilliant colors and good detail in important parts of the picture, you must expose the film correctly. Too much exposure produces slides that are too light and that have pale, washed-out colors. Too little exposure produces dark, murky slides with little texture or detail. Sometimes you may want to deliberately underexpose or overexpose an image to get these effects, but in most cases, the best results come from exposures that are no more than ½ stop over or under the optimum.

Some scenes are more difficult to expose than others. The easiest scenes to expose correctly are those that are evenly lit, with the meter showing little difference in brightness between the darkest and lightest areas (this page, bottom). Scenes like this can vary as much as 1 stop from the optimum exposure and still produce good results.

If a scene is contrasty, however—if it has dark shadows as well as brilliantly lit areas (this page, top)—often no single exposure will be correct for everything in the scene. If the shadowed areas are exposed correctly, the bright areas will be too light; exposing for the bright areas will make the shadowed ones too dark. Try exposing for the most important area, (pages 54–55), then bracketing additional exposures. Pages 90–91 show you how to brighten shadow areas by adding fill light. Pages 70–71 describe how to use dark shadows for dramatic effect. ▪

Bill Gillette

▲

Backlit scenes and other scenes in bright, direct light often have some important areas very light or others very dark or both. You have to choose which area is the most important to you and meter that part of the scene for your exposure.

Richard Frear

Scenes in soft, flat light are the easiest to expose correctly because the lightest areas in the scene are not much brighter than the darkest ones, so there will not be any areas that are too bright or too dark in the final photograph.

COLOR BALANCE:
MATCHING FILM WITH LIGHT SOURCE

The color temperature of light—the mixture of wavelengths of different colors that it contains—varies with different light sources. Daylight, for example, is much bluer than light from an ordinary light bulb. Consequently, different types of color films are balanced to match the color temperatures of specific light sources.

The color temperature of a light source (measured in degrees Kelvin) is a way of describing its color exactly. Color films are made to be used either with daylight, relatively blue in color, or with tungsten light, which is more reddish. The lower the color temperature, the more "warm" red wavelengths there are in the light. Higher color temperatures have more "cool" blue wavelengths.

Film	Color Temperature	Type of Light
	12,000 K and higher	Clear skylight in open shade, snow
	10,000 K	Hazy skylight in open shade
	7000 K	Overcast sky
	6600 K	
	5900-6200 K	Electronic flash
Daylight	5500 K	Midday
	4100 K	
	3750 K	
	3600 K	
	3500 K	
Type A (indoor)	3400 K	Photolamp
Tungsten (indoor)	3200 K	
	3100 K	Sunrise, sunset
	3000 K	
	2900 K	100 watt tungsten bulb
	2800 K	
	1900 K	Candlelight, firelight

Color films are balanced for either daylight or tungsten light. Daylight-balanced films yield the most natural looking colors when shot in daylight or other light that is rich in blue wavelengths. Tungsten-balanced or indoor films produce the best result when used in more reddish light, such as the light from tungsten bulbs. (See illustrations opposite.) Most indoor films are called tungsten-balanced and are designed to be used with light of 3200 K (degrees Kelvin) color temperature; however, they give acceptable results when used with any type of tungsten light. Type A indoor film has a slightly different balance for precise color balance use with high-intensity 3400 K photolamps.

Color balance is important with reversal films. Color slides are made from the film that was in the camera, which should be shot either in the light for which it was intended or with a filter over the lens to adjust the color balance. If this is not done, the resulting slides will have a distinct color cast.

Color temperature is less critical with some films. Color negative films are somewhat tolerant of different color balances because color balance can be adjusted during printing. Some color negative films, such as Kodacolor VR 1000, minimize color balance differences between light sources even more. Black-and-white film can be shot in light of any color temperature. ▪

Alan Oransky

Daylight film in daylight

Tungsten film in daylight

Daylight-balanced films are designed for a light source that is rich in blue wavelengths and low in red, such as daylight (especially near noon), electronic flash, and blue flash bulbs (see illustration above left). If you shot the same scene on tungsten-balanced film, the resulting pictures, particularly slides, would look quite blue (see right). Tungsten films can be used in day-light if an 85 (amber) filter is placed over the lens and the exposure increased by about 1 stop.

Alan Oransky

Tungsten film in tungsten light

Daylight film in tungsten light

Tungsten-balanced films are designed for a light source that is the opposite of daylight: rich in red wavelengths, low in blue—as from household bulbs, photofloods, and clear flash bulbs (see left). If you shot the same scene on daylight-balanced film, the resulting color balance would be reddish-orange (see right). Daylight film can be corrected for tungsten if an 80 (blue) filter is placed over the lens and the exposure increased by about 2 stops. However, light indoors is often too dim for such an increase.

Alan Oransky

Fluorescent light

Fluorescent light plus FL filter

Fluorescent light presents a special problem because the color balance does not match either daylight or tungsten films, and it also depends on the type of fluorescent tube and its age. The light often gives an unpleasant greenish cast to pictures (left). Film manufacturers provide filtration data for different tubes but, practically speaking, the photographer usually doesn't know which tube is installed. Try an FL (fluorescent) filter with 1 stop increase in exposure (right). Daylight film will give a better balance than tungsten film if you use no filter.

CHANGES IN COLOR BALANCE: TIME OF DAY/WEATHER

Have you ever had a picture come out an unexpected color even when you used the correct film? Perhaps a snowy scene in the shade turned out too blue, or a beach scene at sunset looked too orange. If you have, you may know how easy it is to fool the eye when it comes to color balance. Film that is manufactured to render colors accurately in the relatively blue light (high color temperature) at noon, will show colors differently if the color temperature shifts even slightly, for example, as it gets lower and more reddish at sunset.

Color temperature outdoors varies at different times of day and so produces different color balances on film. You'll find these shifts easier to notice if you are looking for them. Before dawn, colors are grayed and monochromatic. As the sun comes up, colors begin to stand out more clearly.

On a sunny day at noon, pictures tend to have clear, bright colors that snap out sharply.

But they appear more reddish than they will later in the day because in the early morning the color temperature of the sun's rays is modified as the rays travel a long distance through the earth's atmosphere.

Daylight-balanced film is designed for the color temperature of sunlight between about 10 A.M. and 2 P.M. During these hours, when the sun is most directly overhead, its rays are modified least by the atmosphere. Colors appear bright, clear, and accurate.

At sunset, the rays are again changed by the atmosphere. Blue rays are filtered out, leaving a surplus of reddish rays that turn color pictures taken at this time a warm, reddish-orange color. This reddish cast may be acceptable with some subjects; wood and skin tones usually appear natural even when the color temperature has shifted considerably to reddish-orange. But other subjects do not work as well; in a snowy winter scene photographed at sunset, the snow may turn an unnatural pink that merely looks odd. At dusk, colors are muted again and gradually become grayed and monochromatic as they were before dawn.

Atmospheric conditions also affect color balance. In the fog, snow, or rain, or on a heavily overcast day, colors are often muted. On these days, the farther away objects are from the camera, the more their colors are toned down. Sometimes a colored object in the foreground appears particularly bright because it is seen against a grayed background. ▪

Fred Figall

At sunset, colors take on a reddish cast. Objects, and even skin tones, may appear quite orange but still pleasing.

Lyntha Eiler

On a foggy day, colors are grayed and softened, particularly in the background. The color balance of pictures will be different under different atmospheric and light conditions.

UNEXPECTED COLORS: BLUE SHADOWS/VERY LONG EXPOSURES

The eye and brain quickly adapt to changes in color balance, especially if they have nothing to compare a color to directly; they tend to see a color as they expect it to be rather than as it is. If you know a dress to be white, your eye and brain see it as white even though it may have a distinctly green cast because of color reflected from grass or trees nearby. Color film is very sensitive to shifts in color balance and can produce unexpected results in the final picture if you are not watching for color casts when you shoot.

Shadow areas often appear bluer in color photographs than we expect them to be. On a sunny day, we tend to see shadows as simply dark, but they are receiving illumination from the indirect and very blue light of the sky. Color portraits taken in the shade (which provides a soft, pleasing modeling of facial features) often have better color balance if a UV (ultraviolet)

or 1A (skylight) filter is used to eliminate some of the excess blue that is not always complimentary to skin tones.

Very long exposures (1 second or longer) cause shifts in color balance that can't be seen or even anticipated very well. During long exposures, film responds more slowly than usual (the reciprocity effect) and you may find your pictures underexposed as a result. In addition, the fact that each of the three layers of film emulsion responds at a different rate causes color balance to shift as well (see opposite).

To prevent underexposure with times of 1 second or longer, increase the exposure as explained on page 58. Color shifts can add interest to sunsets and other pictures, but if you wish to minimize them during long exposures, see the manufacturer's information sheet packed with the film for filters you can use. ▪

A portrait taken outdoors in the shade can have a slightly blue cast (left). A UV (ultraviolet) or a 1A (skylight) filter will remove some of the blue; an 81A (yellow) filter will remove even more (right).

Fredrik D. Bodin

Peter Laytin

Unexpected colors can come from exposures of 1 second or longer. The longer the exposure, the more you are likely to get shifts in the color balance of the picture. A purple sky (below) was created when the photographer left the shutter open for several minutes at night in order to record lightning streaks. At left, a long exposure of a city scene at night produced an intensely yellow picture of a London bridge.

Fredrik D. Bodin

Blue shadows outdoors cause one of the unexpected colors often found in color photographs. The shadows on the snow are obviously blue in the photograph above, but were not so easy to see when the picture was taken. See also photograph opposite, left.

USING DARK SHADOWS

Deep, dark shadows can be a problem, particularly in color slides, because, as explained on page 63, a color slide has only abut ½ stop leeway in exposure. If you underexpose an important area in a color slide by more than ½ stop it will become significantly darker; it may be totally black if underexposed by several stops. But you can use this effect deliberately if you wish, in slides and in other photographs, silhouetting an interesting shape against a lighter background or accenting a brightly lit area that is of interest to you by surrounding it with a mass of dark shadows. ▪

Jerry Howard

▲

A portrait half in shade can be made by metering and exposing for the lit side of the face when the shaded side of the face is much darker.

A silhouette against a ▶ sunset sky was made by metering the brightness of the sky (without including the sun) to calculate the exposure.

Jerry Howard

Silhouetting a subject against the sky can happen unintentionally if you include a bright sky in your meter reading. In the picture below of Natural Bridges National Monument, the photographer deliberately metered the sky for the exposure. The rock formation was several stops darker than the sky and thus was so much underexposed it appeared as almost black. At left, the dark shapes formed by the shaded sides of the building add interest to this city scene.

Fred E. Mang, Jr.

Chapter 5
· SPECIAL TECHNIQUES ·

Bill Gillette

Many special techniques and manipulations are possible with photography. This chapter concentrates on two major areas: close-ups and the use of lens attachments and filters.

Close-ups We are used to seeing and photographing things from viewing distances of several feet or more. But many subjects—a tiny insect, the swirling petals of a flower—have a beauty and intricacy that are seen best from up close. Filling the entire picture with a detail of an object can reveal it in a new and unusual way.

The single-lens-reflex is an excellent camera for close-up work because you view the scene through the lens and see the exact image that the lens does (cameras without through-the-lens viewing show a different view-finder angle than the one the lens projects on the film). Depth of field is usually very shallow when you photograph up close, and an SLR lets you preview which parts of the close-up will be sharp. Through-the-lens metering helps you calculate exposures accurately when using close-up accessories like extension tubes or bellows that decrease the amount of light reaching the film. Pages 80–83 tell more about close-ups and how to make them.

Lens attachments and filters A single-lens-reflex is also a good choice if you want to use lens accessories like cross-screen or multiple-image attachments. As you view the scene you can adjust the attachment right on the lens until you get just the effect you want. The next pages show some of these lens attachments and explain how to use filters that change colors and contrast. ▪

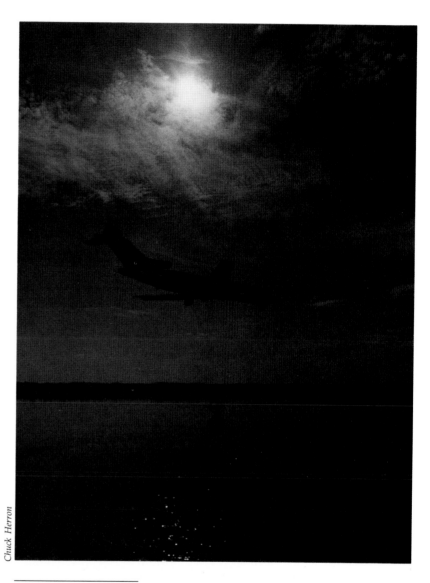

Chuck Herron

Moonlight effect Tungsten-balanced film will produce an image that is too blue for most pictures if it is shot in daylight without a filter to convert the light balance from a daylight color temperature to a tungsten color temperature (as shown on page 65). But if you shoot without a filter and also underexpose the film, you get an effect that looks very much like a moonlit scene. Daylight film with an 80B blue filter produces a similar effect.

USING FILTERS: HOW TO CHANGE FILM'S RESPONSE TO LIGHT

Filters for color photography Filters are often used in color photography to match the color balance of the light to that of the film so that the resulting picture looks more realistic. Using an FL (fluorescent) filter, for example, decreases the greenish cast of pictures taken under fluorescent light (shown on page 65). Or you can use filters to make a color photograph depart from reality, as, for example, in the arctic scene below. Various filters for color photography are listed in the chart opposite.

Filters for black-and-white photography Most black-and-white films are panchromatic—sensitive to all colors to about the extent that the human eye is. However, blue colors tend to record somewhat lighter than we expect them to in black-and-white photographs, and one of the most common uses of filters is to darken a blue sky so that clouds stand out more distinctly (shown opposite). The chart opposite, bottom lists some of the filters used in black-and-white pictures.

Increasing exposures when filters are used Filters work by removing some of the wavelengths of light that pass through them. To compensate for the resulting overall loss of light intensity, the exposure must be increased or the film will be underexposed. Cameras with through-the-lens meters can measure the light through a filter on the lens, and, in most cases, will adjust the exposure as needed. Some types of meter cells may be more sensitive to certain colors than others, so check your owner's manual for special instructions. If you do not have a through-the-lens meter, increase the exposure manually as suggested by the filter manufacturer or as listed in the charts opposite. ▪

Color generates an emotional response and an unexpected color can make an image strikingly unusual. An orange filter was used for this arctic scene.

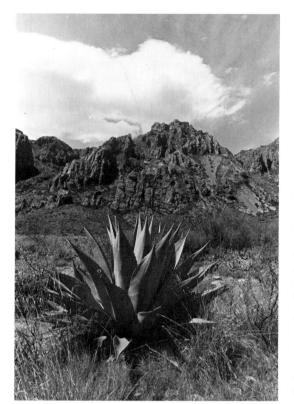

A blue sky may appear very light in a black-and-white photograph because film is sensitive to the blue and ultraviolet light present in the sky.

A deep yellow filter was used on the camera lens for the black-and-white photograph below to darken the blue sky and make the clouds stand out.
▼

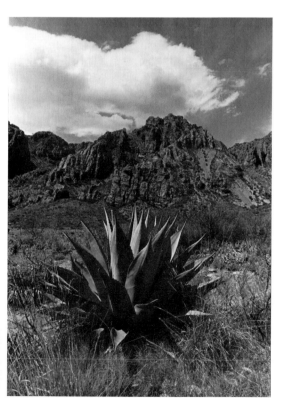

Fredrik D. Bodin

Filters for color film

	Type of filter	Increase needed in exposure
To get a natural color balance with daylight-balanced film exposed in tungsten light.	80A (blue) with photolamps	2⅓ stops
	80B (blue) with ordinary tungsten bulbs	2 stops
To get a natural color balance with tungsten-balanced film exposed in daylight.	85B (amber) with daylight-balanced film	⅔ stop
	85A (amber) with Type A film	⅔ stop
To get a natural color balance with fluorescent light.	FL-B with tungsten-balanced film	1 stop
	FL-D with daylight-balanced film	1 stop
To reduce the bluishness of light on overcast days or in the shade. To penetrate haze. Used by some photographers to protect lens.	1A (skylight)	No increase
	UV (ultraviolet)	No increase
To decrease bluishness more than 1A or UV.	81A (yellow)	⅓ stop
To decrease the red-orange cast of light at sunset and sunrise.	82A (blue)	⅓ stop
To balance film precisely as recommended by film manufacturer.	CC (color compensating): R (red), G (green), B (blue), Y (yellow), M (magenta), C (cyan)	Varies
To experiment with color changes.	Any color	Varies

Filters for black-and-white film

		Type of filter	Increase needed in exposure
To darken blue objects to:	Natural effect	8 (yellow)	1 stop
Make clouds stand out against blue sky.	Darker	15 (deep yellow)	1⅓ stops
Reduce haze in distant landscapes.	Very dark	25 (red)	3 stops
Make blue water darker in marine scenes (effect shows if sky is blue).	Darkest	29 (deep red)	4 stops
To increase haze for atmospheric effects in landscapes. To lighten blues to show detail, as in flowers.		47 (blue)	2⅔ stops
To lighten reds to show detail, as in flowers.		25 (red)	3 stops
To lighten greens to show detail, as in foliage.		58 (green)	2⅔ stops
To make the range of tones on panchromatic black-and-white film appear more like the range of brightnesses seen by the eye.		8 (yellow) with daylight	1 stop
		11 (yellow-green) with tungsten light	2 stops

LENS ATTACHMENTS: POLARIZATION, STARS, AND OTHER EFFECTS

A polarizing screen can remove reflections. If you have ever tried to photograph through a store window and seen more of the reflections from the street than whatever you wanted to photograph on display inside the store, you know how distracting unwanted reflections can be. Using a polarizing screen is a way to eliminate some of these reflections. The screen eliminates or decreases reflections from glass, water, or any smooth non-metallic surface.

When shooting landscapes, using a polarizing screen makes distant objects clearer. The effect is strongest when you are shooting at a 90° angle to the sun.

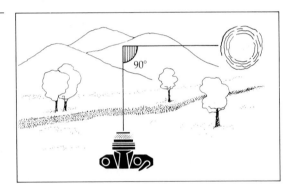

A polarizing screen removes reflections from surfaces such as glass (see illustrations opposite). The screen works best at a 30°–40° angle to the reflecting surface.

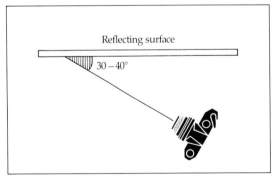

Landscapes can be sharper and clearer with a polarizing screen. Light reflected from minute particles of water vapor or dust in the atmosphere can make a distant landscape look hazy and obscured. A polarizing screen will decrease these minute reflections and allow you to see more distant details. It may also help to make colors purer and more vivid by diminishing unwanted coloring such as reflections of blue light from the sky.

The screen works best at certain angles to your subject (see diagrams this page). The screen attaches like a filter to the front of the camera lens. With an SLR you can look through the viewfinder and adjust the screen until you get the effect you want. An exposure increase of 1 to 2 stops is usually required.

Special effects with lens attachments Stars of light in your photographs? Multiple images of a clump of wildflowers recorded several times on the negative or slide with just one exposure? In addition to the filters that change tone or color, other lens attachments manipulate or change the image itself. They can add drama to an otherwise ordinary picture, blur details to make an image soft and romantic, or change a scene in other unusual ways. If you take one or two along in your camera bag you might find uses for them that you hadn't expected. See the lens attachments illustrated on the following pages. ▪

▲

A cross-screen lens attachment, sometimes called a star filter, put the bright stars of light in the photograph above. An eight-ray attachment created the rays around the sun and its reflections from the airplane. Other cross screens produce four, six, or other numbers of rays.

Reflections are a distracting element in the top photograph if the goal is to show the display inside the shop window. A polarizing screen on the camera lens removed most of the reflections in the bottom photograph so that the objects inside can be seen clearly. You may not always want to remove reflections, however; notice how the people reflected in the top photograph can be seen as an interesting addition to the picture.

LENS ATTACHMENTS
FOR SPECIAL EFFECTS

		Without attachment	**With attachment**

Soft focus

Softens details and can make bright highlights shimmer and gleam.

Spot lens

A sharp central field becoming progressively hazy at the edges. For emphasizing details of a subject.

Prism 3X (triangular)

Triangular prism without a central image.

Prism 3X (parallel)

Multiple prism with three parallel fields. Reproduces the subject side by side, tilted, or one above the other.

Prism 5X

A central field and four marginal sectors give a five-image reproduction.

Prism 6X

Image is reproduced six times with five images arranged around a central field.

Color prism 3X (parallel)

Three parallel fields with colors changing gradually from yellow to green, blue, and purple.

Color prism 6X

Pentagonal arrangement of five fields around the center field, with same color changes as above.

Prism 6X (Parallel)

The subject is repeated six times with one large image and five adjacent, parallel ones.

Close-up prism

Makes a close-up of a small object while at the same time doubling it— side by side, one above the other, or at parallel angles.

Split field or bifo

Part of the filter surface is a close-up lens and the rest is clear glass. Thus objects at close range (approx. 10 in. or 24 cm) and those far away can be focused sharply at the same time.

Eccentric spot lens

An off-center split field allows both a distant object and a very close one to be focused sharply.

Cross screen (four-ray, six-ray, eight-ray)

Each point source—a point of bright light or bright reflection— radiates rays of light.

Spectra (4X, 8X)

Each point source of light radiates starlike beams in three spectral colors. Especially visible in night scenes.

Spectra (2X)

Parallel beams of spectral colors emanate from every point light source.

Spectra (48X)

Petal-shaped spectral beams around each point light source.

Spectra (72X)

Color spectra emanate from each point light source.

Courtesy of B+W Filterfabrik

CLOSE-UPS:
BIGGER AND BETTER

Close-up equipment Shown opposite are the different types of close-up equipment you can use to produce a larger-than-normal image on your negatives. All of them do the same thing: they let you move in very close to the subject you are photographing.

Whether to use a camera support like a tripod depends on what and where you are photographing. You will be more mobile without one—ready to photograph an insect that has just alighted on a branch or to get down very close to a low-growing wildflower. However, close-up exposures are often longer than normal, and a tripod helps prevent blur caused by camera motion with a slow shutter speed. Also, a tripod lets you compose your pictures precisely, perhaps keeping the scene framed just as you want it while you meter it or arrange the lighting.

Increased exposures for close-ups Placing extension tubes or bellows between the lens and the camera body lets you move in close to a subject, but the farther the lens gets from the camera, the dimmer the light that reaches the film. Beyond a certain extension the exposure must be increased or the film will be underexposed. A camera that meters through the lens increases the exposure automatically if compatible extension tubes or bellows are used. But if your camera does not meter through the lens or if the close-up attachment breaks the automatic coupling between lens and camera, you must increase the exposure manually. To do so, follow the recommendations given by the manufacturer of the tubes or bellows, or see the chart, opposite, below. Close-up lenses (see opposite) do not require an exposure increase. ∎

Close-up terms The closer your camera is to a subject, the larger the image on the film. A close-up is any picture taken from closer than normal to the subject—specifically, when the image on the film ranges from about 1/10 life size (1:10) to as big as life size (1:1). Macrophotography generally refers to an image on film that is anywhere from life size (1:1) to as big as ten times life size (10:1). Photomicrography, photographing through a microscope, is usually used to get a film image larger than 10:1.

Life size (1:1) on film, enlarged to 2X life size here

1/10 life size (1:10) on film, enlarged to 1/4 life size here

Alan Oransky

A close-up lens attaches to the front of a camera lens and lets you focus up close without using extension tubes or bellows. Close-up lenses come in different strengths (diopters); the stronger the diopter, the closer you can focus and the larger the image. Close-up lenses are relatively inexpensive, small, and easy to carry along in your camera bag, and they do not require additional exposure as do extension tubes or bellows. However, image quality may not be as good as with other close-up methods.

A macro lens is your best choice for sharp close-ups. It produces a very sharp image at close focusing distances, whereas an ordinary lens produces its sharpest image at normal distances. A macro lens's mount can be extended more than that of an ordinary lens, which means that even without the use of extension tubes or bellows it can produce an image up to about half life size (1:2).

Reversing a lens produces a sharper image when the lens is used very close to the subject. At a short focusing distance an ordinary lens is being used under conditions for which it was not designed and, as a result, image sharpness decreases; reversing the lens improves sharpness. An adapter ring couples the lens to the camera in reversed position.

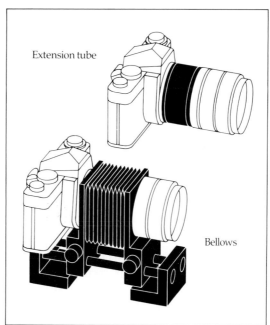

Extension tube

Bellows

Extension tubes and bellows fit between the lens and the camera. They increase the distance from the lens to the film; the greater this distance, the closer you can bring the lens to the subject. Extension tubes come in graduated sizes that can be used in various combinations to make close-ups of different sizes. A bellows is more adaptable than fixed-length tubes because it can be expanded to any length. Using either tubes or bellows requires increasing the exposure, as explained opposite.

Exposure increase needed for close-ups*

If the long side of the area being photographed measures in inches	11	5⅛	3¼	2¼	2	1¾	1⅜	1
in cm	28	13	8.5	5.75	5	4.5	3.5	2.5
Open lens aperture this number of f-stops	⅓	⅔	1	1⅓	1½	1⅔	2	2½
Or multiply exposure time by	1.3	1.6	2	2.5	2.8	3.2	4	5.7

*Increase applies to a lens of any focal length used with a 35mm camera.

MORE ABOUT CLOSE-UPS

Depth of field is shallow in close-ups. At very close focusing distances, as little as an inch or less of the depth in the scene may be sharp, and the closer the lens comes to the subject, the more the background and foreground go out of focus. Accurate focusing is essential or it may miss the subject altogether. Small apertures help by increasing the depth of field but they also increase the length of the exposure time. It may be necessary to use a tripod and, if you are photographing outdoors, to shield your subject from the wind to prevent its moving during the exposure.

Making the subject stand out from the background Since a close-up is usually one small object or part of an object, rather than an entire scene, it is important to have some way of making the object you are photographing stand out clearly from its background. If you move your camera around to view the subject from several different angles, you may find that from some positions the subject will blend into the background, while from others it becomes much more dominant. You can choose your shooting standpoint accordingly.

Shallow depth of field can be an asset in composing your picture. You can use it to make a sharp subject stand out distinctly from an out-of-focus background. Tonal contrast of light against dark, the contrast of one color against another, or the contrast of a coarse or dull surface against a smooth or shiny one can also make your close-up subject more distinct.

Depth of field is very shallow when a photograph is made close to a subject. Only the insect's head and upper body are in focus; the front and rear legs and even the tips of the antennae are not sharp. The shallow depth of field can be useful: since the sharply focused parts contrast with the out-of-focus areas, the insect stands out clearly from the foreground and background.

Fred Ward

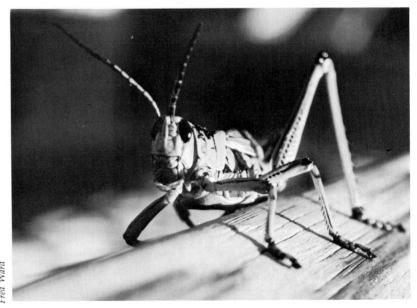

Lighting close-ups outdoors   Direct sunlight shining on a subject will be bright, and you can use smaller apertures for greater depth of field. But direct sunlight is contrasty, with bright highlights and very dark shadowed areas. Fill light helps to lighten the shadows if this is the case (pages 90–91). Light that comes from the back or side of the subject often enhances the subject by showing texture or by shining through translucent objects so they glow. In the shade or on an overcast day, the light is gentle and soft, good for revealing shapes and details.

Lighting close-ups indoors   You have more control over the lighting if you are arranging it yourself indoors, but stop for a moment and think about just what you want the lights to do. For flat subjects the lighting is not critical just so long as it is even. Two lights of equal intensity, each at the same distance and angle from the subject, will illuminate it uniformly.

If you want to bring out texture, one light angling across the subject from the side will pick out every ridge, fold, and crease. With a deeply textured object, you may want to add a second light close to the lens to add fill light so that important details are not lost in shadows.

Flash can be added to increase the light level if you need to use a smaller aperture or faster shutter speed, and you can also use flash as a fill light. Using the flash very close to the subject may make the light too bright; draping a handkerchief over the flash (out of the way of the camera lens) will soften the light and decrease its intensity. ▪

Stanley Rowin

Cross lighting brought out the texture and volumes of this ear of corn. The main light angled across the subject from one side, while a weaker fill light close to the camera lightened the shadows.

Chapter 6
· LIGHTING ·

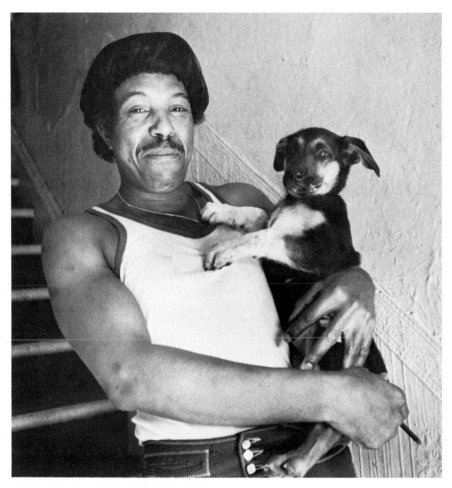

Jonas Dovydenas

Changes in lighting will change your picture. Outdoors, if clouds darken the sky or you change position so that your subject is lit from behind or you move from a bright area to the shade, your pictures will change as a result. Light changes indoors, too: your subject may move closer to a sunny window or you may turn the overhead lights on or decide to use flash lighting.

Changes in lighting affect the exposure of your film and the color balance of the light (important with color films). Just as important, the light can affect the feeling of the photograph so that the subject appears, for example, brilliant and crisp, hazy and soft, stark, romantic, or any of many other ways. If you make a point of observing the light on your subject, you will soon learn to predict how it will look in your photographs and you will find it easier to use existing light to arrange the lighting yourself to give just the effect you want. ▪

Look at the light on your subject. Soft, diffuse light bouncing in from outdoors softly lit a man and his dog just inside a doorway, opposite. A father and daughter on a crabbing expedition (right) are darkly silhouetted against reflections from water. Light can be as important a part of the picture as the subject itself.

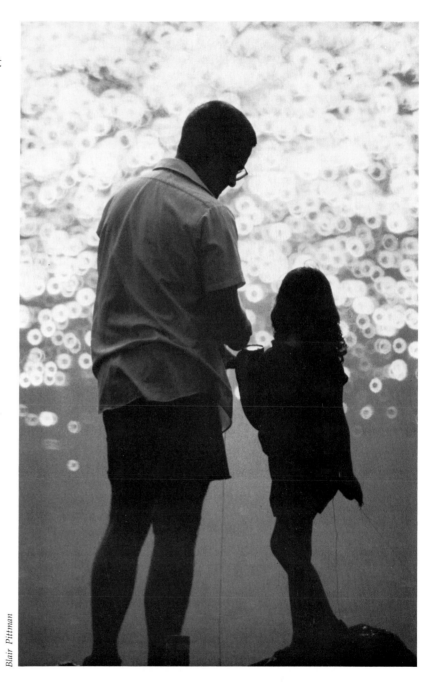

Blair Pittman

QUALITIES OF LIGHT: FROM DIRECT TO DIFFUSED

Whether indoors or out, light can range from direct and contrasty through many intermediate levels to diffuse and soft. Here's how to predict where you will find these different qualities of light and how they will look in your photograph.

Direct light is high in contrast. It creates bright highlights and dark shadows with sharp edges. Photographic materials, particularly color slides, cannot record details in very light and very dark areas at the same time; so in a slide the colors in directly lit areas will appear brilliant and bold while shadowed colors may turn out almost black. If you are photographing in direct light, you may want to add fill light (pages 90–91) to lighten shadows. Because the direct light probably will be quite intense, you can use a small aperture to give plenty of depth of field, a fast shutter speed to stop motion, or both, if the light is bright enough. The bright sun on a clear day is a common source of direct light. Indoors, a flash or photolamp pointed directly at your subject (that is, not bounced off another surface) also provides direct light.

Diffused light is low in contrast. It bathes subjects in light from all sides so that shadows are weak or even absent. Colors are less intense than they are in direct light and are likely to be pastel or muted in tone. Since the light will be less intense than direct

light, you might not be able to use a small aperture with a fast shutter speed. The sun on a heavily overcast day casts diffused light because the light is coming from the whole dome of the sky rather than just from the small disc of the sun. Indoors, diffused light can be created with a very large source of light used close to the subject (such as light bounced into a large umbrella reflector) plus additional fill light.

Directional/diffused light is intermediate in contrast. It is partly direct and partly diffused. Shadows are present, but they are softer and not as dark as in direct light. Colors are bright and more likely to be accurately rendered in both highlights and shadows. You will encounter this type of light on a cloudy day when the sun's rays are somewhat scattered so that light comes from the surrounding sky as well as from the sun. A shaded area, such as under trees or along the shady side of a building, can have directional/diffused light if the light is bouncing onto the scene primarily from one direction. Indoors, a skylight or other large window can give this type of light if the sun is not shining directly on the subject. Light from a flash or photolamp can also be directional/diffused if it is softened by a translucent diffusing material placed in front of the light or if it is bounced off another surface like a wall or an umbrella reflector. ▪

Direct light

Bill Marr

Diffused light

Michelle Bogre

Directional/diffused light

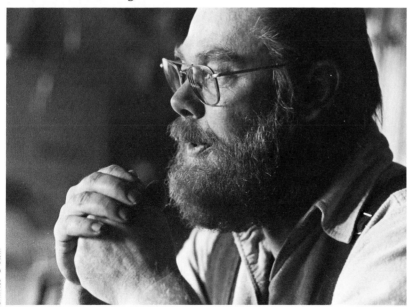

Charles O'Rear

Light changes—from place to place and at different times of day. Compare the qualities of the light in these portraits. Direct light (above, left)—hard edged and contrasty. Diffused light (above, right)—indirect and soft. Directional/diffused light (left)—softer-edged shadows.

THE MAIN LIGHT: THE STRONGEST SOURCE OF LIGHT

The most realistic and usually the most pleasing lighting resembles daylight, the light we see most often: one main source of light from above creating a single set of shadows. Lighting seems unrealistic (though there may be times when you will want that) if it comes from below or if it comes from two or more equally strong sources that produce shadows going in different directions.

Shadows create the lighting. Although photographers talk about the quality of light coming from a particular source, it is actually the shadows created by the light that can make an image harsh or soft, menacing or appealing. To a great extent the shadows determine the solidity or volume that shapes appear to have, the degree to which texture is shown, and sometimes the mood or emotion of the picture.

The main light, the brightest light shining on a subject, creates the strongest shadows. If you are trying to set up a lighting arrangement, look at the way the shadows shape or model the subject as you move the main light around or as you change the position of the subject in relation to a fixed main light.

Direct light from a 500-watt photolamp in a reflector was used for these photographs, producing shadows that are hard-edged and dark. Direct sunlight or direct flash can produce the same effects. The light would be softer if bounced onto the subject from another surface, like an umbrella reflector, or if it were diffused. Fill light (see next pages) will lighten the shadows. ▪

Front lighting Here the main light is placed close to the lens, as when a flash unit attached to the camera is pointed directly at the subject. Fewer shadows are visible from camera position with this type of lighting than with others, and, as a result, forms seem flattened and textures less pronounced. Many news photos and snapshots are front-lit because it is simple and quick to shoot with the flash on the camera.

High 45° lighting If the main light is moved high and to the side of the camera, not precisely at 45° but somewhere in that vicinity, shadows model the face to a rounded shape and emphasize textures more than with front lighting. This is often the main light position used in commercial portrait studios; fill light would then be added to lighten the shadows.

Fredrik D. Bodin

Side lighting A main light that is at about a 90° angle to the camera will light the subject brightly on one side and cast shadows across the other side. When the sun is low on the horizon at

sunset or sunrise, it can create side lighting that adds interest to landscapes and other outdoor scenes. Side lighting is sometimes used by portrait studios to dramatize a subject.

Top lighting With the light directly overhead, long dark shadows are cast into eye sockets and under nose and chin, producing an effect that is seldom appealing for portraits. Unfortunately, top lighting is

not uncommon—outdoors at noon when the sun is overhead or indoors when the main light is coming from ceiling fixtures. Fill light to open up the shadows will help.

Back lighting Here the light is moved around farther to the back of the subject than it is in the photograph above. If the light were directly behind the subject the entire face would be in shadow with just

the hair outlined by a rim of light. Outdoors, bright light that comes from behind the subject can silhouette it unless fill light from the front is used to lighten the shadows.

Bottom lighting Lighting that comes from below looks distinctly odd in a portrait. This is because light on people outdoors or indoors almost never comes

from below. This type of light casts unnatural shadows that often create a menacing effect. Some products, however, like glassware, are effectively lit from below.

THE FILL LIGHT:
TO LIGHTEN SHADOWS

A sunny day is an inviting time to go photographing. But, particularly for portraits, bright, direct sunlight may create harsh, contrasty shadows that come out too dark in the final photograph. This can be corrected by adding fill light to lighten the shadows.

Fill light outdoors It is easier to obtain a pleasant expression on your subject's face in a sunlit outdoor portrait if your subject is lit from the side or from behind and is not squinting directly into the sun. However, this position may make the shadowed side of the face too dark. To decrease the contrast between the lit and shadowed sides of the face, fill light from a reflector or flash unit can be added, as illustrated below. Fill light is also used outdoors for close-ups of flowers or other relatively small objects in which the shadows would otherwise be too dark.

When do you need fill light? Photographic materials, particularly color slides, can successfully record color and texture in either brightly lit areas or in deeply shadowed ones, but not in both at the same time. So if important shadow areas meter more than one or two stops darker than highlight areas, consider whether adding fill light will improve your picture, especially if you are shooting color slides. The fill light should not overpower the main light but should simply raise the light level of shadow areas. ▪

Alan Oransky

Front light The man's face is illuminated brightly by sunlight shining directly on it. But facing into the sun almost guaranteed an awkward squint against the bright light.

Back light Here he faces away from the sun and has a more relaxed expression. However, most of his face is now in shadow; it is dark in this print and would be even darker in a color slide. Increasing the exposure would lighten the shadowed side of his face but would make the lit side very light.

Back light plus fill light Here he still faces away from the sun, but to lighten the shadows the photographer has added fill light from a small flash unit on the camera.

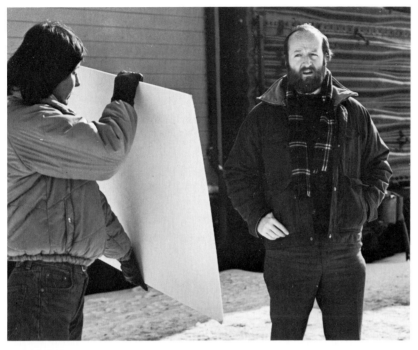

Using a reflector for fill light A large light-colored cloth or card can lighten shadows in back-lit or side-lit portraits by reflecting back some of the illumination from the main light. For color photographs, the reflector should be neutral in color so that an unwanted color is not cast on the subject. Sometimes nearby objects will act as natural reflectors, for example, sand, snow, water, or a light-colored wall.

At left, an assistant holds the reflector for the photographer, but in many cases the reflector could simply be propped up. The closer the reflector is to the subject, the more light it will reflect into the shadows.

For a portrait, meter the lit side of the face to determine the basic exposure. Then try to angle the reflector to add enough fill light so the shadowed side of the face is about one stop darker than the sunlit side.

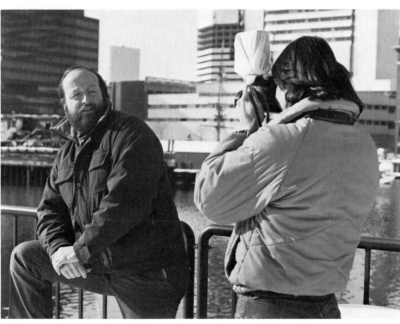

Alan Oransky

Using flash for fill light To lighten the shadows on the man's face, the photographer at left has attached a flash unit to her camera. If the flash light is too bright it can overpower the main light and create an unnatural effect. To prevent this, the photographer has draped a handkerchief over the flash head to decrease the intensity of the light. She could also have stepped back from the subject or, with some units, decreased the light output of the flash.

See your owner's manual for instructions on how to set your camera and flash for fill lighting. In general, you will need to decrease the brightness of the flash on the subject until it is about one stop less than the basic exposure from the sun. Position the fill light close to the camera (attached to the camera is fine) so as not to cast a second set of shadows that will be visible from camera position.

USING ARTIFICIAL LIGHT: PHOTOLAMP OR FLASH

Artificial light sources let you bring your own light with you when the sun goes down or you move inside into a darkened room or you need just a little more light than is available naturally. Artificial sources are consistent and never go behind a cloud just when you're ready to take a picture. You can manipulate them to produce any effect you want—from light that looks like natural sunlight to underlighting that is seldom found in nature. Different sources produce light of different color balances, an important factor if you are using color films. See pages 64–65 for more about color balance and films.

Continuously burning lamps such as photolamps and quartz lamps plug into an AC electrical outlet. Since they let you see how the light affects the

subject, they are excellent for portraits, still lifes, and other stationary subjects that give you time to adjust the light exactly. Determining the exposure is easy: you meter the brightness of the light just as you do outdoors. The color balance of these lights is matched to two types of color film: the lamps emit either a 3200 K color temperature for use with tungsten-balanced color film or 3400 K for Type B film.

Flashbulbs are conveniently portable, powered by small battery units. Each bulb puts out one powerful, brief flash and then must be replaced. Press photographers not so many years ago could be followed by the trail of spent flashbulbs they left as they discarded a bulb after each shot. Flashbulbs are still in use for some special purposes and are also used with snapshot cameras that accept flashcube or flip-flash units. Flashbulbs are blue coated for use with daylight-balanced color film or are clear for tungsten-balanced film. Bulbs that put out only infrared light are also available.

Electronic flash or strobe is now the most popular source of portable light. Though initially more expensive than flashbulbs, it offers many repeated flashes without the need of replacing the bulb, so it is ultimately more economical. Power can come from either battery packs or an AC outlet. The color balance of electronic flash is best with daylight-balanced color film. Flash (from either an electronic flash or a flashbulb) is fast enough to freeze most motion; flash is therefore a good choice when you need to light candid or unposed shots.

(A) Flashbulb and reflector
(B) Flashcube
(C)(D) Electronic flash units
(E) Photolamp

Flash must be synchronized with the camera's shutter so that the flash of light occurs when the shutter curtains are fully open. Only shutter speeds of 1/60 sec. or slower synchronize with electronic flash (up to 1/125 sec. with certain shutters). At faster shutter speeds the shutter curtains open only part of the way at any time and only part of the film would be exposed. See your owner's manual for details on how to set your camera.

Automatic flash units measure the amount of light reflected back from the subject during the flash, then terminate the flash when the exposure is adequate. Even if you have an auto-matic unit, there are times when you will want to calculate the flash exposure yourself, such as when the subject is very close to the flash or very far from it and so is not within the automatic flash range.

Determining your own exposure with flash is different from the procedure used with other light sources. The flash of light is too short to measure with an ordinary light meter. Instead, the intensity of the light is measured by the distance of the flash from the subject, and the aperture is set accordingly (see below). Changing the shutter speed (within the acceptable range) does not affect the exposure. ∎

Guide number is 80 with this flash unit used with ASA 100 film. Distances in these examples are measured in feet.

5 ft.   10 ft.   20 ft.

$$\frac{\text{Guide number}}{\text{Distance from flash to subject}} = \text{f-stop}$$

$$\frac{80}{5} = 16$$

$$\frac{80}{10} = 8$$

$$\frac{80}{20} = 4$$

f/16   f/8   f/4

To set your own flash exposure, set the aperture according to how far your subject is from the flash: divide the distance from flash to subject into the guide number (a rating for the flash when used with a specific film speed); the result is the f-stop that should be used.

Flash units have a calculator dial that will do the division for you: dial in the film speed and the distance from the subject, and the dial will show the correct f-stop.

Notice that the farther the subject is from the flash, the dimmer is the light that it receives and so the larger the aperture opening that is needed to maintain the same exposure.

MORE ABOUT FLASH

Flash is easy to use for portrait lighting: the flash of light exposure is so fast that you don't have to worry about the subject moving during the exposure—particularly important with children—and you can expose at the instant your subject has the expression you want. Light from flash is so quick (1/1000 sec. or shorter) that you can't really see what the subject looks like when lit. However, with a little practice you can predict the qualities of light that are typical of different flash positions. Shown on the opposite page are some simple lighting setups for portraiture.

A few cautions with flash If you have the flash close to the lens and the sitter is looking directly at the camera, you may find that your subject's eyes appear red or amber in a color picture. This is because light is reflecting from the blood-rich retina inside the eye. The effect can be easily prevented by having the subject look slightly to one side or by holding the flash away from the camera. If your subject wears eyeglasses, this will also prevent bright reflections from them. Reflections from shiny backgrounds can be avoided with flash by shooting at an angle to them. ▪

Unwanted reflections When using flash you may fail to notice bright, distracting reflections caused by light bouncing back from reflective surfaces like shiny walls, mirror, or glass.

To avoid reflections with flash, shoot at an angle to highly reflective surfaces or move the flash to one side. The light will be reflected off at an angle instead of returning to the camera.

Alan Oransky

Direct flash on camera is simple and easy to use because the flash is attached to the camera. However, the light shining straight at the subject from camera position tends to flatten out roundness and gives the photograph a rather harsh look.

Direct flash off camera—usually raised and to one side—gives more roundness and modeling than does flash on camera. A special extension (synchronization or synch) cord lets you move the flash away from the camera. To avoid a shadow on the wall, move the subject away from it or raise the flash more.

Alan Oransky

Flash bounced from the ceiling onto the subject gives a softer, more natural light than direct flash. Usually about 2 stops more exposure is needed than with direct flash from the same distance. Light can also be directed into an umbrella reflector and then bounced onto the subject.

Flash bounced from a side wall onto the subject gives a soft, flattering light. The closer the subject is to the wall, the more distinct the shadows on the subject will be. To avoid a shadow on the back wall, move the subject away from it.

Chapter 7
· SEEING LIKE A CAMERA ·

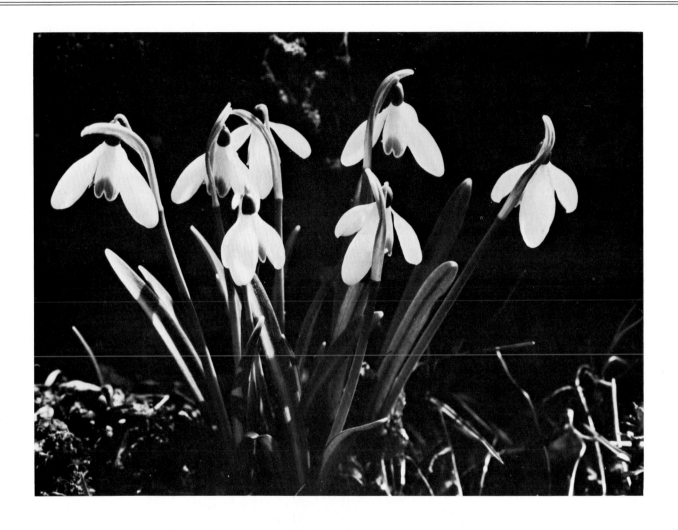

Pictures translate the world we see. If you have ever had a picture turn out to be different from what you anticipated, you know that the camera does not "see" the way a human sees. For example, in a black-and-white photograph the colors we see in the world are translated into shades of gray, but even color film does not record colors exactly the way the eye sees them, and a color print can alter colors even more.

The way we see contrast is also different from the way film responds to it. When we look at a contrasty scene, the iris of the eye continuously adjusts to different levels of brightness by opening up or closing down. In a photograph the contrast between very light and very dark areas is often too great for the film to record them both well in the same picture, so some areas may appear overexposed and too light or underexposed and too dark. Motion, sharpness, and other elements also can be similar to what we see in the original scene, but never exactly the same.

The creative part of photography is that you can choose the way you want the camera and film to translate a scene. You decide whether you want traffic to blur into a stream of lights. You decide whether you want the sky to be almost white or showing detail in clouds. You decide whether you want the flowers brightly lit against a very dark background. More about your choices—and how to make them—on the following pages. ▪

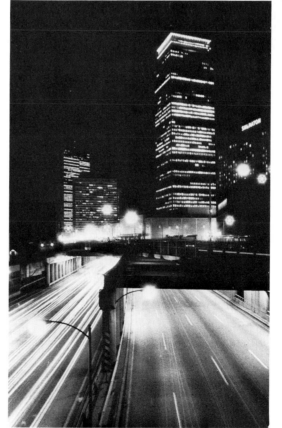

David A. Morrison

Choices During a 15 sec. exposure, lights on moving automobiles streaked (left). A shorter exposure would have made the streaks shorter and the roadway even darker. Above, the sky and water were brighter than the fishermen and their boat. More exposure would have made the whole scene lighter, revealing more of the people, but with the sky almost white. Opposite, the background was much darker than the flowers. With more light on the background or with more exposure, the background would have been more visible, but the flowers would not have stood out so strongly.

WHAT'S IN THE PICTURE:
THE EDGES OR FRAME

One of the first choices to make with a photograph is what to include and what to leave out. The image frame, the rectangle you see when you look through the viewfinder, shows only a section of the much wider scene that is in front of you. The frame crops the scene—or, rather, *you* crop it—when you decide where to point the camera, how close to get to your subject, what angle to shoot at—in other words, what to include in your picture.

Decide before you shoot whether you want to show the whole scene (or as much of it as you can) or whether you want to move in close for a detail. You can focus attention on something by framing it tightly or you can step back and have it be just another element in a larger scene. When you look through the viewfinder, imagine you are viewing the final print or slide. This will help you frame the subject better. The tendency is to "see" only the subject and ignore its surroundings. In the final print, however, the surroundings and the framing are immediately noticeable.

You can also change framing later by cropping the edges of a picture either when you print it yourself or when you send it to a lab to be printed. Many photographs can be improved by cropping out distracting elements at the edges of the frame. But if you are making slides, it is best to crop when you take the picture. Although you can duplicate a slide and change its cropping then, it's easier to frame the scene the way you want it when you shoot. ∎

The edges of a picture, the frame, surround and shape the image. Look around the edges at how the frame cuts into some objects or includes them in their entirety. How could different framings change these pictures?

Fredrik D. Bodin

Lyntha Eiler

You can frame the central subject of a picture with other parts of the scene. Showing the instruments surrounding the fiddler at center, while cropping out most of the musicians themselves, focuses attention on the fiddler.

WHAT'S IN THE PICTURE: THE BACKGROUND

Seeing the background When you view a scene, you see most sharply whatever you are looking at directly, and you see less clearly objects in the background or at the periphery of your vision. If you are concentrating on something of interest you may not even notice other things nearby. But the lens does see them, and it shows unselectively everything within its angle of view. Unwanted or distracting details can be ignored by the eye looking at a scene, but in a picture they are evident. To eliminate a distracting background, you can shoot the background out of focus (see page 104) or change your angle of view as in the photographs below. Interesting juxtapositions that usually go unnoticed—except in a photograph—are one of the pleasures of photography, as in the picture opposite. ▪

A distracting background of a building is an unnecessary element in this portrait. The woman and child also seem rather a small part of the picture.

A plainer and better background resulted when the photographer simply walked around to one side and changed the angle from which he shot the subject. The photographer also moved in closer so that the people would occupy a larger area of the picture.

Fredrik D. Bodin

John White

If you look at the background of a scene as well as the principal subject of interest, you may find some good combinations. Here, the leader of a high school band frames the rest of the band with her outstretched arm. The camera records everything within its angle of view and can make the relation between a foreground object and a background one more important than we might otherwise notice.

DEPTH IN A PICTURE: THREE DIMENSIONS BECOME TWO

Photographs can seem to change the depth in a scene. When you translate the three dimensions of a scene that has depth into the two dimensions of a flat photograph, you can expand space so that objects seem very far apart, or you can compress space so that objects appear to be crowded close together. For example, compare the two photographs below. You can compress the buildings in a city (opposite) into flat planes to look almost as if they were pasted one on top of the other, or you can give them exaggerated height. Pages 34–35 explain more about how to control perspective effects like these that can change the way a photograph shows depth. ▪

Two lenses of different focal lengths gave two very different versions of the same scene from the same position: a short-focal-length lens (top) expanded the space; a long-focal-length lens (bottom) compressed it. Neither of the lenses actually changed anything in the scene. The short-focal-length lens simply included nearby objects as well as those that were farther away. The part of the scene shown in the bottom photograph is exactly the same within the wider view of the scene shown in the top photograph.

Alan Oransky

Dan McCoy

Two perspectives of the same city Buildings appear to tower to great heights when you look down on them (bottom). The closer any object is to your eye or to the camera, the bigger it appears to be, so the building looks larger at the top than at the bottom because the camera was closer to its top stories than to its bottom ones. Sections of buildings seen from the side seem to lie one right on top of the other (top). Clues that might indicate the actual space that exists between the buildings are all excluded from the scene.

DEPTH OF FIELD: WHICH PARTS ARE SHARP

We are usually not aware that we focus our eyes on only one distance at a time while objects at all other distances are not as sharp. Our eyes automatically adjust their focus as we look from one object to another. You might look at the butterfly in the scene opposite, bottom and not notice that you are not seeing the girl just on the other side of the window as clearly as you see the butterfly. But in a photograph, differences in the sharpness of objects at different distances are immediately evident. Such differences can be distracting or can add interest to the photograph.

Controlling the depth of field   In some photographs you have no choice about depth of field (the area within which all objects will appear acceptably sharp). For example, in dim light or with slow film or under other conditions, the depth of field may have to be very shallow. But usually you can control the depth of field to some extent, as shown on pages 30–31. It is not necessarily better to have everything totally sharp or the background out of focus—or to follow any other rules, but it is important to remember that in the photograph you will notice what is sharp and what isn't. ▪

Landscapes are often photographed with everything sharp from foreground to background. The entire landscape is important, not any single part of it. If you had been standing by the camera when this picture was taken, each part of the scene would have looked sharp to you. You wouldn't have noticed that your eyes were actually focusing sharply first on the fence in the foreground, then refocusing on the house in the middle distance, then focusing again on the mountains in the background.

P. E. Farnes

Duane Dailey

Throwing the background out of focus is one way to make a busy background less distracting. The eye tends to look first at the objects in a photograph that are the sharpest, and here the interesting part of the picture is the woman roping the calf, not the fence and the next corral in the background.

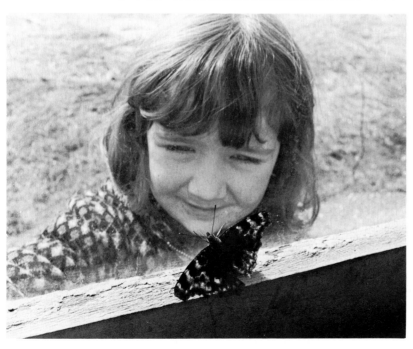

Byron Schumaker

The most important part of the picture is usually—but not always—the one that is focused most sharply. With the butterfly very sharp and the girl slightly out of focus, the relationship between the two of them is emphasized even more than it would be if both of them were equally sharp.

TIME AND MOTION
IN A PHOTOGRAPH

A photograph is a slice of time. Just as you select the section that you want to photograph out of a larger scene, you can also choose the section of time you want to record. You can think of a photograph as slicing through time, taking a wide slice at a slow shutter speed or a narrow slice at a fast shutter speed. In that slice of time, things are moving, and, depending on the shutter speed, direction of the motion, and other factors dis-

cussed earlier (pages 10–11), you can show objects frozen in mid-movement, blurred until they are almost unrecognizable, or blurred to any extent in between. How would you have photographed the rodeo scene (opposite, top)—sharp, as it is, or blurred to show the jolting of the bull? How about the boxers (below)—blurred and streaked or sharp and crisp to show their exact stances? ▪

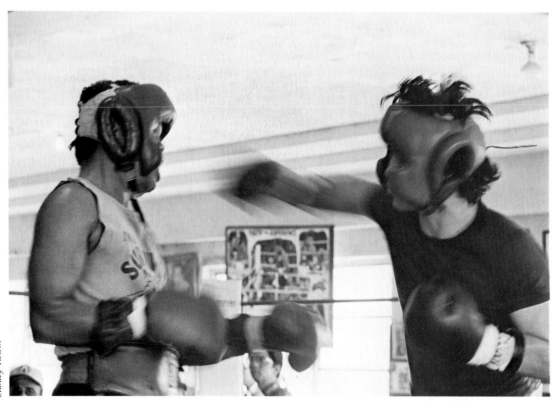

Stanley Rowin

A slow shutter speed blurred the boxers' fists, which were moving, while their torsos, which were relatively still, are sharper.

John White

A fast shutter speed froze the motion of the bull, men, hat, and dust. With bright sunlight and a high film speed, the photographer was also able to use a small aperture so that everything is sharply focused from foreground to background.

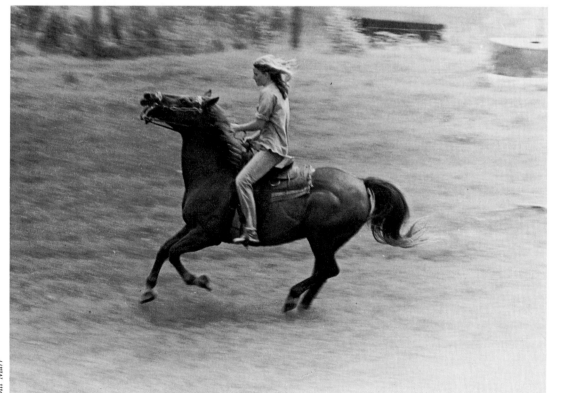

Bill Marr

Panning, moving the camera in the direction that the subject is moving, is another way to show motion. The moving subject is relatively sharp while the surrounding scene is blurred.

PHOTOGRAPHING CHILDREN:
AT THEIR LEVEL

Children are probably the most photographed subjects in the world, but all too often photographers look down on them from adult height. If you can get down to children's level by kneeling, sitting, or doing whatever you have to, you and your photographs can participate more intimately in their world. You can also put children more at ease if you and your camera are at about their height rather than looming over them. ▪

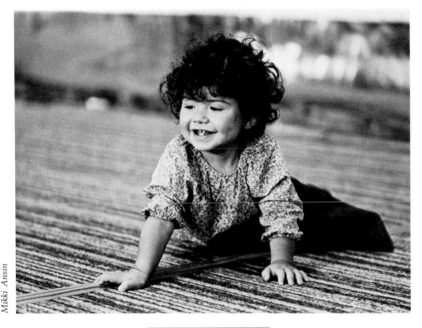

Mikki Ansin

Shooting from a low level may show more of the background than if you shot down on a subject from above. Use a small aperture if the background adds interest to the picture and you want it sharp. Use a large aperture if you want the background out of focus and less noticeable.

Fredrik D. Bodin

Fredrik D. Bodin

A person looking into the camera lens can be an effective way of conveying direct contact with your subject. These children seem at ease with the photographer and involved with the picture-making process. If you are physically at their level, children (and adults) may be more receptive to your presence than if you stare down at them so that they have to crane their necks to look up at you.

Thomas A. Burns

PHOTOGRAPHING CHILDREN: WHILE THEY ARE OCCUPIED

Photographing children when they are busy doing something besides being photographed is a good way to capture expressions that are natural and spontaneous. It pays to be familiar with the camera's controls so that you can operate them easily and quickly. Telling a child to "hold still" while you make last-minute adjustments is likely to produce a wooden smile at best. ▪

Fredrik D. Bodin

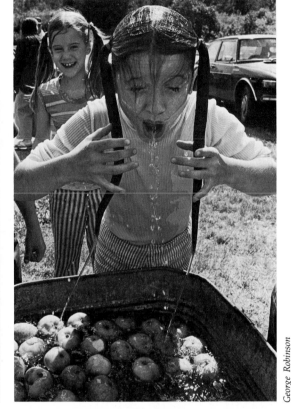

George Robinson

Take a moment to think ahead and adjust the camera's controls to advantage while children are engrossed in some activity. If you expect a subject to move fast (as in the pictures this page), set your shutter to a fast speed if you want action to be sharp in the photograph. If action is slower or if the subject pauses from time to time, you can use a slower shutter speed and still get a sharp picture.

Ronald Parson, Jr.

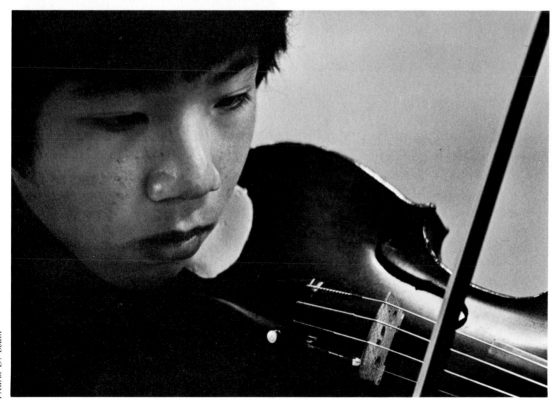

Fredrik D. Bodin

AN ENVIRONMENTAL PORTRAIT

People shape the space around them, and photographing them in their own environment—where they live or work or wherever they have established a corner of their own—can tell much more about them than just a straight head-and-shoulders portrait. How the subject sits or stands—quietly on her porch or tense with the effort of a power lift—adds an extra dimension to his or her character and to the portrait.

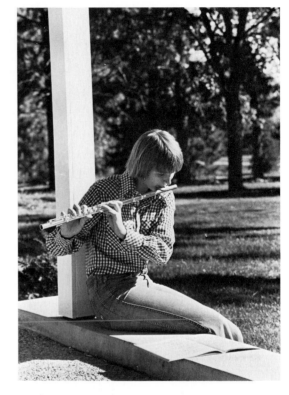

A flute player seems completely at ease and relaxed as she practices on her porch. Sunshine, grass, and trees add a pleasant, peaceful note.

A power lifter focuses all her attention on her lift and dominates the attention of everyone else in the room as well.

Ken Robert Buck

A violin maker has surrounded himself with his product in addition to his tools.

◄ A baker proudly displays the results of his work in front of the table on which he had kneaded and shaped the loaves a short time earlier.

▲ Four generations of a Vermont farm family pose in front of their dairy operation. Their work clothes make the picture realistic and believable, as if they had just stepped away from their chores.

PHOTOGRAPHING THE LANDSCAPE/CITYSCAPE

How do you photograph a place? There are as many different ways to view a scene as there are photographers. Most important for you: What do you want to remember? What is the best part of the place for you? Do you want many buildings from a distance or just one structure up close? Is it the landscape as a whole that is interesting or some particular part of it, like the fences, opposite? How does a place speak to you?

After photographing a standard view of New York City as seen from Brooklyn, across the East River (below), the photographer turned his attention to the nearby Brooklyn Bridge, whose pattern of stone arches and cables creates shapes reminiscent of a Gothic cathedral (right).

Fredrik D. Bodin

Thomas A. Adler

A. L. Weeks

Lyntha Eiler

Landscapes are not always ready-made for the photographer, with dramatic mountains or stormy skies to add interest. Even so, a scene that at first may seem rather ordinary can make an appealing picture if you stop for a moment and look at what is actually present. Here, fences not only draw the eye of the viewer into the scene, but have interesting shapes of their own.

GUIDE TO EQUIPMENT AND ACCESSORIES

Olympus Camera Corp.

This section prepared by Lista Duren

35mm SINGLE-LENS-REFLEX CAMERAS

Although many single-lens-reflex (SLR) cameras are capable of producing excellent pictures, different models can produce different results in certain situations. If you are buying a camera, you will want to choose equipment that fits the kind of photography you like to do.

The exposure system is an important factor to consider when you are comparing how easy it will be to use different cameras. The viewfinder display and other features can also affect your final choice.

Exposure systems A manual camera gives you exposure information so that you can set any shutter speed and aperture you want. An automatic camera sets one or both of these controls for you.

Manual (match-needle) cameras have an indicator in the viewfinder to tell you when the camera controls are set for the proper exposure. This indicator may be a moving needle or a colored light which you match, center, or otherwise align by changing the aperture and/or shutter speed. You can tell at a glance whether the camera is set for normal exposure, underexposure, or overexposure, so you can adjust the controls accordingly.

Automatic cameras take over part of the needle-matching required with manual systems. They operate in one or more of the automatic modes described below; the camera sets the shutter speed or aperture or both automatically to give you a correct exposure.

Aperture-priority mode You set the aperture and the camera chooses the shutter speed to give correct exposure. This gives you direct control over depth of field. You can indirectly control shutter speed (and thus the appearance of moving objects) by changing the aperture; for example, opening the lens to a wider aperture automatically increases the shutter speed.

Shutter-priority mode You choose a shutter speed and the camera selects the appropriate aperture automatically for correct exposure. This mode is advantageous for photographing moving objects because you can set the shutter

The Olympus OM-1, a match-needle camera, can be used with many different lenses and accessories. It is lightweight and compact..

Olympus Camera Corp.

The multimode Canon A-1 allows you to set either the shutter speed or the aperture and the camera will automatically adjust the other control for correct exposure. In its programmed mode the camera will set both shutter speed and aperture for optimum exposure. Programmed automatic exposure is also possible with Canon Speedlite flash units. With the camera set on manual, the built-in meter will provide a suggested exposure and you can set both the shutter speed and the aperture yourself.

Canon, Inc.

speed fast enough to freeze motion or slow enough for the movement to record on the film as a blur. To change the aperture in this automatic mode, you must change the shutter speed; for example, changing to a slower shutter speed will stop down the lens to a smaller aperture.

The Pentax MG is a compact camera designed for automatic operation. In its automatic aperture-priority mode, you set the aperture and the camera sets the correct shutter speed for normal exposure. The shutter operates manually at B setting for time exposures and at 1/100 sec., the flash synchronization speed. It will continue to operate at these settings when camera batteries are dead.

Pentax Corp.

Programmed mode Designed so the camera selects both shutter speed and aperture, this mode is ideal in situations when things are happening so fast that you don't have time to adjust the camera yourself. It can be helpful for beginners; in ordinary lighting situations even the first pictures will be well exposed.

Multimode cameras allow you to switch the mode of operation depending on the situation. For example, if the camera has both shutter-priority and aperture-priority modes, you can use shutter-priority to photograph fast-moving objects to freeze or blur the action. When depth of field is more important, you can use the camera in the aperture-priority mode. Switch to programmed mode, if your camera has that option, when you want the camera to set both controls.

Manual operation Some cameras allow you to set both the aperture and shutter speed yourself if you want to. Others are designed primarily for automatic operation and do not have a fully manual mode in which you can set any shutter speed and aperture combination yourself.

Metering systems Almost all 35mm SLRs have a built-in through-the-lens metering system—a light-sensitive cell (or cells) that measures the amount of light reaching the film. The light reading or the recommended exposure is indicated in the camera's viewfinder by a needle or other display.

Most cameras have center-weighted meters that read the entire scene but give greater emphasis to the center of the picture, where the main point of interest is most likely to be. Center-weighted meters are more apt to produce properly exposed pictures than meters that read all parts of the scene equally.

In certain lighting situations, such as backlit scenes where even center weighting may not give a completely satisfactory exposure, you can move in close to take a meter reading from a specific part of the scene. Many cameras have an exposure lock that will hold the correct setting even when you return to your original position to shoot.

Viewfinder information Cameras display information in their viewfinders so that you can set the controls without taking the camera away from your eye. The viewfinder display may include indicators for correct exposure, overexposure, or underexposure; shutter speed and aperture settings; a camera shake warning at slow shutter speeds; a manual mode indicator; focus confirmation; a flash-ready light; a flash distance check; a battery check; or other data. This information may be in the form of needle indicators, light-emitting diodes (LEDs), digital displays, audible signals, or a combination of these. It should be easy to read and understand, even in low light, but it should not intrude on the scene you are composing in the viewfinder.

Most viewfinders show 90 to 97% of the image that will appear on the film. The amount that is missing in the viewfinder is about the same amount that will be covered by a slide mount or, in the case of a framed print, by an overmat.

In a needle-centering display, the camera controls are set for correct exposure when the needle is centered between + (overexposure) and – (underexposure).

A match-needle display has a needle that moves according to the light meter reading and a second "lollipop" needle that moves when you change the aperture or shutter speed settings. The camera is set for correct exposure when the two needles are aligned.

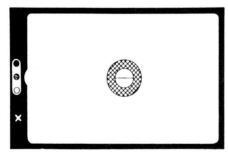

In this stop-go version of an LED display, a green diode lights up when the shutter speed/aperture combination chosen provides enough light for good exposure. Red diodes indicate that the chosen settings will underexpose or overexpose the picture

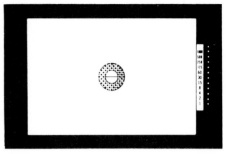

This light-emitting diode (LED) display lights up next to the shutter speed and/or aperture to which the camera is set. When you change an exposure setting, a different diode lights up to indicate the matching setting. Some displays have diodes that light up to warn of under- or overexposure when you choose an aperture or shutter speed for which the camera can't find a correct matching setting.

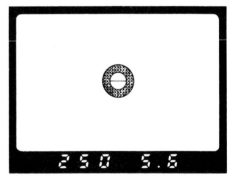

A digital display is easy to read even in dim light because the liquid crystal display actually lights up the shutter speed and aperture numerals.

Other features vary among different SLR cameras.

Size and weight vary quite a bit, from light and compact to somewhat heavier and bulkier. The camera you choose should be a convenient size for you to hold and operate, and it should be light enough to carry around comfortably.

The focusing screen on which you view the image as you focus it may have a microprism spot, split-image focusing, or other features. Try focusing different cameras in both dim and bright light to see if any are significantly easier for you to use.

Range of shutter speeds Some cameras offer a choice of shutter speeds from 1 sec. to as fast as 1/4000 sec., and others extend the range into multisecond exposures. If you expect to photograph under extremely dim or extremely bright light, this range could be a consideration.

An electronic shutter is controlled by an electronic timing circuit and is often found on cameras with automatic exposure systems. It is quieter than a mechanical shutter, usually offers a wider range of shutter speeds, and often can be operated at intermediate speeds between the normal settings. However, electronic operation is dependent on a battery, and when the battery fails the shutter may operate at only a few speeds or quit altogether. You can and should carry extra batteries with you but it is preferable if the shutter will still operate mechanically at least at one speed without batteries.

Nikon, Inc.

The Nikon FE is a compact, automatic camera that operates in the aperture-priority mode. (It is shown here with flash and motor drive.) It features an exposure compensator, which allows you to intentionally under- or overexpose, an exposure memory lock, which allows you to expose at a distance according to a meter reading taken close up, and a manual override, which switches the operation to manual control. A wide range of lenses and accessories are available to fit it.

Depth-of-field preview In normal operation, the camera lens remains at its widest aperture until the moment of exposure. This provides the brightest possible viewfinder image, but it means that you view the picture with the shallowest depth of field. A depth-of-field preview lever stops the lens down to the selected aperture so that you can see how much of the scene is in focus in front of and behind the main subject.

Multiple-exposure capability Cameras have safeguards that prevent accidental double exposure. Some cameras also have a multiple exposure lever that allows you to hold the film in the same place for two or more exposures, when you want to do so.

Flash capability A hot-shoe bracket on top of the viewfinder mounts the flash and connects it to the shutter release. Most cameras have a flash synchronization speed between 1/60 and 1/100 second, a few have a speed of 1/200. Faster sync speeds enable you to use your flash for fill light outdoors, where you may want a relatively fast speed for other reasons.

Focus confirmation and automatic focus are currently available on only a few cameras. The electronic focusing mechanism lets you know by a special viewfinder display whether or not your subject is in focus and which way to turn the focusing ring to bring it into focus. When an automatic focus camera is equipped with a special motorized lens, it will automatically bring the subject into focus.

Lenses and accessories For major-brand SLRs you can purchase interchangeable lenses of different focal lengths and accessories such as close-up equipment, interchangeable viewfinders and focusing screens, motor drive, or a fitted case. Before you buy, be sure that the range of lenses and accessories available is adequate for the kind of photography you expect to do. See the next page for more information on SLR accessories.

THE SLR SYSTEM

The SLR system Professional photographers often need highly specialized equipment for different assignments; synchronized flash for fashion photography, perspective correction for architecture, remote control for nature studies, and so forth. All of these requirements certainly could not be met by one simple camera, and buying a different camera for each kind of photography you want to do would be enormously expensive. However, a single-lens-reflex camera is part of a *system* of interchangeable lenses and other accessories that can be used to adapt one basic camera body to any number of specific uses.

Professional-model SLRs Several camera manufacturers produce a "professional" camera body that is the most flexible camera in the manufacturer's system. It has the largest number of interchangeable parts and can be used with the largest selection of accessories. The professional model is a sturdy camera designed for hard, long use.

Lenses The range of lenses generally includes several focal lengths from fisheyes and extreme wide-angle lenses to normal focal lengths to extremely long telephotos. Most systems also include zoom lenses that offer a continuous choice of focal lengths and macro lenses for close-up work. Some manufacturers also make lenses such as shift lenses, which correct perspective in architectural photography, and medical lenses with close focusing capability and built-in lights.

The focusing screen supplied with most cameras has a split-image focusing spot surrounded by a microprism collar, centered on a ground-glass field. However, you may find that for some kinds of photography, another type of screen is better. For example, macro and extreme telephoto lenses are easier to use with brighter-than-usual focusing screens, architectural shift lenses work best with a screen that has a grid, and so forth. Consequently, a variety of interchangeable screens are available for system cameras. Some cameras must be taken to a professional repairperson to have the screen changed. Others are built so that you can change it yourself.

The viewfinder supplied with an SLR is a pentaprism which allows you to view through the camera lens at eye level. Interchangeable finders or easy-to-attach finder accessories include right-angle finders, waist-level finders, focusing magnifiers, and viewfinder eyepieces corrected for near- or farsightedness.

Close-up accessories There are a number of accessories that make it simpler to photograph small objects at close range. (See information on close-ups on pages 80–83.) Most of these accessories can be used with any camera in the manufacturer's line, though some combinations will interrupt automatic exposure circuitry and must be used with manual exposure.

Copy stands provide steady support for camera and lights when you are doing close-up work. Slide copiers attach directly to the camera body so you can make full-sized duplicates or negatives.

Some manufacturers also make a line of equipment for photomicrography. There are adapters and stands for attaching the camera to the microscope as well as the eyepiece adapters, viewing magnifiers, and special exposure meters.

Nikon, Inc.

Nikon's F3 is part of their professional system. It gives you a wide choice of interchangeable lenses, viewfinders, focusing screens, motor drive, flash, and close-up equipment. The viewfinder contains full exposure information: aperture and shutter speed, over- and underexposure indicators, and, when you are using a compatible flash unit, a flash ready light that also acts as a signal of correct flash exposure.

Motor drive advances the film automatically as soon as a picture is taken, so the camera is always ready for the next shot. It can be useful in action photography when you need to keep your full attention on the subject.

Motor drive may also be set to trip the shutter repeatedly at predetermined intervals—a few frames per second for recording action, or at longer intervals for time-lapse photography. Because rapid exposures put extra strain on the camera mechanisms, some units lock the viewing mirror in the up position when operating at top speed. The disadvantage of this feature is that when the mirror is up, your view through the camera is blacked out.

Remote control units allow you to operate the camera from a distance, a feature that is especially convenient for photographing wildlife.

Motor drive units can use up a 36-exposure roll of film in a hurry, so interchangeable camera backs are available to carry bulk film magazines. Motor drives are battery powered and some will operate on AC or DC current as well.

Power winders are similar to motor drives but tend to be slower (perhaps advancing 2 frames per second at top speed). Although they often have fewer options, they are less expensive and more compact.

Other SLR system equipment includes filters, grips for holding the camera in a well-balanced position with long lenses or heavy attachments, lens caps, cases, flash units, and hardware for attaching one or more different accessories to the camera.

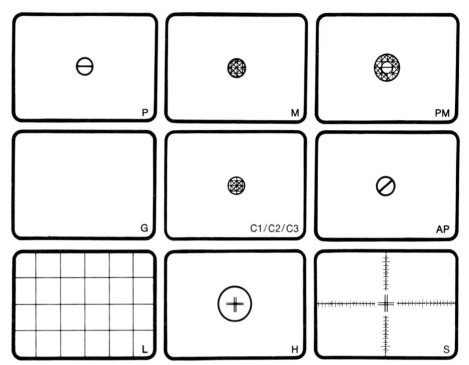

Interchangeable focusing screens are available for some cameras. This selection from Minolta fits their XK series cameras. For general photography: Type P—matte fresnel field with split-image rangefinder spot; Type M—matte fresnel with microprism spot; Type PM—matte fresnel with split-image plus microprism; Type G—matte fresnel only; Types C1/C2/C3—clear fresnel with microprism. For precise alignment: Type L—matte fresnel with etched grid. For high magnification work: Type H—matte fresnel with central clear circle and cross mark; Type S—clear fresnel with central cross plus measuring scales.

Olympus Camera Corp.

The Olympus Motor Drive 1 shown here on the OM-1 camera shoots up to 5 frames per second without mirror lock-up. Batteries and switches are in the M.18V Control Grip 1. The bulk film magazine carriers on either end of the camera are part of the 250 Film Back which accommodates up to 250 exposures and has a built-in exposure counter.

LIGHTING EQUIPMENT

Electronic flash has almost completely replaced the use of flash bulbs for reasons of economy and convenience. Major considerations when choosing a flash unit are size and power, type of operation, and kind of batteries.

Size and power Pocket-sized units are about 3 x 4 x 1½ inches and large units are about the same size as a camera. (Large units with a separate power supply will not be discussed here because they are ordinarily used only by professionals.) In general, large units are more powerful and emit a brighter flash of light than small ones. Power is indicated on each unit by a list of guide numbers, each one corresponding to a different film speed (ASA rating). If you choose one film speed for comparison, the unit with the highest guide number is the most powerful.

A pocket-sized flash is easy to carry and light enough that the camera can still be easily managed with the flash in place. For many situations it will give sufficient illumination, but for photographing subjects at long distances or providing a high level of illumination with diffuse or bounced flash, a large unit that puts out more light is more suitable.

Manual vs. automatic operation On manual flash units you have to estimate your camera-to-subject distance and then use the calculator on the flash unit to determine the f-stop for correct exposure. An automatic flash has a photoelectric sensor which regulates the length of the flash once you have set the f-stop. If you want to alter the normal light level for unusual effects, automatic units can also be operated manually.

Batteries used in flash units are either nickel-cadmium or alkaline, and some units will run with either kind. Either will provide the unit with adequate power. Alkaline batteries cost less initially but they wear out and must be replaced. Nickel-cadmium batteries are cheaper in the long run because they don't wear out. But you do have to recharge them regularly by plugging them into an AC outlet, and recharging may take from 1 to 12 hours. Interchangeable battery clips, available for many units, allow one set of batteries to recharge while the other is in the flash.

Other features may also affect your decision when buying a flash unit.

Recycle time is the time it takes a unit to accumulate enough charge for the next flash after a picture has been taken. It can range from less than a second to many seconds so it is important to consider if you will want to take several shots in rapid succession, with a motor drive unit, for example.

Thyristor circuitry An energy-saving device. The closer the subject is to the camera, the less light is needed to illuminate the subject adequately. However, the flash unit always builds up the maximum charge that it can—more than it needs if the subject is close. Ordinary units dissipate the unused energy, but thyristor circuitry recycles it back into the flash's power system. This means that when you photograph with less than the maximum output, you get more flashes per charge and a shorter recycling time,

and you may not have to recharge the battery as often. Thyristor circuitry is an important feature if you intend to use the flash along with a motor drive.

Bounce flash Some units have a tilting flash head which allows you to bounce light off a ceiling or other reflector. If you want an automatic unit with bounce flash capability, buy a unit in which the sensor remains pointed at the subject when the flash head is tilted away.

A dedicated (or designated) flash, when used with the specific make and model camera for which it was designed, will usually set the correct shutter speed for synchronization with flash and will provide a signal in the camera's viewfinder when the flash is fully charged and ready to fire. It may also warn you of improper mounting, incorrect exposure, an incompatible f-stop, or that the camera is not set in the automatic mode.

Minolta Corp.

Minolta's Auto Electroflash 128 is a lightweight, clip-on flash unit that has a movable head for bounce flash use. The unit operates automatically or manually and has a flash distance check lamp that lights up to signal correct exposure.

Vivitar Corp.

Vivitar's Model 285 Zoom/Thyristor Electronic Flash provides variable angle light coverage for 35mm camera lenses with focal lengths from 28 mm to 105 mm via a built-in optical zoom/bounce flash head. Optional accessories include filter kits, a bounce umbrella attachment, various power sources, shutter release cords, a remote flash trigger, case, quick release pistol grip with camera brackets, cable release, and extension cords.

Accessories Some flash units have an entire system of accessories such as adapters, color filters, remote sensors to trigger a second flash unit, and battery chargers. If you expect to be doing extensive work with flash at some point, you may want to purchase a unit for which you can buy accessories as you need them.

Photolamps Household incandescent bulbs may be used with different kinds of reflectors to create many different lighting situations. But they have two drawbacks: they often can't provide bright enough light for shooting indoors, and because they have a low color temperature (around 2500 K), they lend a yellowish cast to color photographs.

Bulbs developed specifically for photographers give brighter light at a higher color temperature (3200 or 3400 K). Consequently it is easier to provide light that is bright enough indoors, and if these bulbs are used with a color film that is balanced for tungsten, the color in the final photograph will look natural.

Photofloods are tungsten bulbs made in several sizes from 250 watts to 500 watts. Less expensive than other photographic bulbs, they have a rather short lifetime (3–10 hours). There are three kinds available. Two of them are designed to be used with a metal floodlight reflector (like the one shown on this page). One is a clear bulb for direct light, the other is a bulb with a reflective coating on the front to bounce light out of the reflector. The third kind, the reflector flood, is not used with a metal reflector since it has its own painted-on reflective coating on the back. Using the regular photofloods with reflectors is advantageous if you need the support of the reflector to attach filters or shading devices. Otherwise, the reflector flood is adequate and more convenient to carry.

Quartz-halogen lamps (also called quartz-iodine) are tungsten lamps with an active gas surrounding the filament to prolong lamp life. They cost more than photofloods initially but have a much longer lifetime (about 75 hours). They are more powerful than photofloods but smaller, so the reflectors are also smaller and easier to carry. The lamps maintain a constant color temperature over the life of the bulb whereas other bulbs grow dimmer and produce a more reddish light the longer they are used.

Larson Enterprises, Inc.

Umbrella reflectors are used to bounce light onto the subject. The light—flash or photolamp—is pointed at the reflector instead of at the subject. The Reflectasol umbrella is made by Larson Enterprises. It comes in several colors: silver, translucent, and white, which produce no color change in the light; silver blue, which balances tungsten light to 5600 K for use with daylight film; or gold, which adds a warm skin tone when the subject is illuminated with daylight or strobe.

Smith-Victor Corp.

Reflectors for photographic lights vary from the simple aluminum reflector that screws onto a socket-and-clamp assembly to the Smith-Victor unit shown here, which features a swivel base, a mounting stud to fit on a light stand, a vented housing so you can handle the light without getting burned, and a rim-mounted holder for filters and shading devices.

Smith-Victor Corp.

Barn doors are lightweight black panels that can be folded in front of the bulb to control the size of the beam of light reaching the subject and to prevent the light from shining directly into the lens. They are shown here on a quartz studio light made by Smith-Victor Corporation.

Tripods

A tripod is helpful whenever you need to provide a stable support for the camera: for shooting long exposures, for self-portraits, for steadying a long lens or other heavy attachment that might wobble if it were hand held, or for just making sure the image is as sharp as possible.

A unipod, clamp, grip, or brace can be used for steadying a camera and can be more convenient than a tripod to carry and to set up. But if you want an independent support that ensures camera stability, there's no substitute for a tripod.

Size and weight Tripods come in all sizes from tiny tabletop models to 8 ft. giants that require a ladder for focusing; but the most widely used varieties are 3–5 ft. tall with sectioned telescoping legs so you can use only part of the height if you want a lower-than-eye-level view. The legs are generally round or C-shaped in cross-section and ½–1½ inches in diameter. Although the very lightweight models are usually too shaky for a single-lens-reflex camera, the sturdiest ones provide more support than you need unless you're using a very long lens or other heavy accessory, and they are quite heavy and bulky to transport. Choose one that is stable enough, when fully extended, to support your camera with its heaviest accessories and make sure it is easy to carry when folded.

Tripod feet come in several different styles. Rubber tips are sensible for use indoors or on surfaces such as sidewalks. Metal spikes ensure a good grip in grass or soil. If you work in both situations, look for rubber collared feet that retract to expose metal spikes.

The head is the movable part of the tripod that holds the camera in place. The two popular kinds are the ball-and-socket joint and the pan-and-tilt head, and many tripods will take either kind.

The ball-and-socket joint is compact, lightweight, and inexpensive. It also allows maximum versatility of movement because the camera is free to move in any direction once the joint is loosened, and it takes only one quick operation to place the camera at exactly the angle you want. However, this free movement can also be frustrating; the camera tends to flop to one side if the joint isn't tight; consequently, making slight adjustments in the camera position can be a tedious procedure.

Tripod The Stitz Model 3U/BA three-section channel-leg elevating tripod has a three-way tilting head, a geared center column, and rubber feet that retract to reveal ground spikes.

Stitz Corp.

Bogen Photo Corp.

Clamps Whenever there is a railing, door, or sturdy piece of furniture available at the proper height for the camera, a clamp can provide a perfectly adequate support. Styles vary from a simple C-clamp (like a carpenter's clamp) with padded jaws and a ball-joint head to the Bogen Super Clamp 3025 shown here. The head on this clamp, with three rotating joints to control pan, tilt, and swing, is also available as a tripod head.

Pan-and-tilt heads, which are heavier, bulkier, and more expensive than ball-and-socket joints, provide separate control over horizontal and vertical movement. Most heads will pan (turn to left or right) in a full circle and tilt (move forward or back) until the camera is pointing up or down. Some heads have a third control for cross-tilt (also referred to as side swing), which is a sideways movement in the vertical plane. This is advantageous when the tripod is on uneven ground and you want to make a quick adjustment to level the camera with the horizon. Some cross-tilt controls allow the camera to swing a full 90° for vertical pictures.

A quick-release connector, found on some tripods, lets you remove the camera quickly. The connector is attached to the camera with a conventional tripod screw and snaps into the head of the tripod.

Stitz Corp.

Very small "tabletop" tripods are easy to carry and much more convenient than large ones if you want to raise the camera only a short distance. The Stitz tripod shown here doubles as a chest support to steady the camera for hand-held shots.

Center columns The basic tripod consists of the head attached directly to the three-legged structure. For more flexibility you could buy one with a head attached to a center column for raising and lowering the camera short distances (major height adjustments should be made by adjusting the legs).

Manually operated columns have a friction-tightened clamp that holds the column where you set it. The mechanism is simple and lightweight, but the column may slip or turn as you are adjusting the height.

Geared columns allow a smooth up-and-down movement without any camera rotation. They are heavier and more expensive than manual ones. Some center columns may be used upside down to hold the camera near the ground, and others are designed to take two cameras.

An additional feature on some tripods is a joint that allows the center column to be used horizontally, vertically, or at any angle in between.

Camera straps and cases

Although 35mm SLR cameras are lightweight and rugged, they do have sensitive inner workings that can be easily damaged by a fall. Accidental damage can be prevented by using a good strap. Simple neck straps and wrist straps are widely available as are straps for holding the camera close to the body so you can move freely without worrying that the camera might hit something.

Cases are also a necessity to protect equipment from scratches, dirt, and moisture. There are individual hard or soft cases made for almost all pieces of photographic equipment. Cases for carrying a whole set of equipment vary from gadget bags to foam-lined suitcases. An inconspicuous carrying case may help to deter theft. With this thought in mind, some photographers prefer to wear a jacket with many pockets rather than carry a case at all.

Necksaver, Inc.

Straps Necksaver Inc. makes several different kinds of straps for holding one or two cameras close to the body. The Harnastrap shown here keeps the camera from swinging around when you bend over. The bottom connection can be released quickly when you want to use the camera.

Tenba/Weinreb Design

Soft cases Because camera equipment is a prime target for theft, and many pieces are small and easy to lose, it's safest not to set things down while you're shooting. A compartmentalized gadget bag with a shoulder strap like this Tenba P795 by Tenba/Weinreb Design makes it easy to find what you need and to keep everything on your person while you're taking pictures.

Berkey Marketing Companies

Hard cases A padded case provides excellent protection for shipping or carrying equipment. This System Case by the Zero-Halliburton Division of Berkey Marketing Companies has a lightweight aluminum shell, deep foam padding, and an interlocking closure to seal against dust and moisture.

SLIDE AND PRINT STORAGE AND DISPLAY

Slide storage and display Slides are easy to store and take up very little space, but in order to find the one you want quickly, you'll need a good storage system. The most common methods of storage are projector trays, slide file boxes or drawers, and clear plastic slide sheets.

Slide viewing equipment can help you sort and evaluate transparencies quickly. Options include hand or table viewers that show one slide at a time and slide sorters or light tables that allow you to compare and organize large quantities of slides. Some have ordinary incandescent bulbs which give your slides a slight yellowish cast, and others have daylight-type bulbs for exact color rendition.

Print storage and display Prints are easily scratched and damaged, so care must be taken in storing and displaying them. Whether you use albums, storage boxes, or frames will depend on the kind of pictures you take and who will be viewing them.

Albums Prints of friends and family are often displayed in albums with plastic-covered pages to protect them from dust and handling. Many albums have pockets to hold snapshot-sized prints, or 5 x 7 or 8 x 10 enlargements. Others have self-adhesive pages so that you can arrange a combination of different-sized prints on the same page.

Matting and mounting Large numbers of prints are most easily stored in boxes. But if you have prints that you show to people often, you will probably want to mount them on a backing, and perhaps add an overmat, which is cut from a large piece of mat board or rag board and has a "window," or opening, through which the print is viewed. Mounting provides a wide border around the print, making it easier to view and to handle, and it adds stiffness to the print to keep it from getting bent.

There are several ways to attach a print to the backing to keep it flat. Dry mounting is a heat process in which a wax-impregnated sheet bonds the print and backing together. Mounting adhesives that do not require heating are also available. Or you can attach a print to the backing with photo corners (which can be hidden by the overmat).

Agfa-Gevaert, Inc.

Slide viewers This battery-powered Agfa-scope 100 made by Agfa Gevaert magnifies the image to about three times its original size. It has incandescent illumination and a screen large enough for only one person at a time to view the slide. Larger models are designed for viewing by several people at once. Macbeth makes a large tabletop viewer with daylight-colored illumination.

Keystone Ferrule & Nut Corp.

Boxes and drawers The Kenco metal slide file shown here is a convenient way to store and transport large numbers of transparencies. It holds 300 slides and has an index in the lid that you can code to help you locate slides quickly. Another system for storing slides at home is a stacking unit with slide-file drawers. You can add new units to the system as you need them.

Logan Electric Spec. Mfg. Co.

Slide sorters and light tables The translucent backlit surface of slide sorters and light tables makes it possible to look at many slides at once. The Logan Electric 1080 Super Slide Sorter and Viewer shown here has a slanted viewing surface with ridges for holding up to eighty slides. Illumination is provided by an ordinary incandescent bulb. Light tables come in a variety of sizes and many are equipped with daylight-type fluorescent tubes.

Plastic Sealing Corp.

Plastic sheets Notebooks with transparent plastic sheets, like this one made by Plastic Sealing Corp., are convenient for storage because you can hold the sheet up to the light and see at a glance which slides you have. Similar plastic sheets are made to fit in file drawers. For even larger numbers of slides there are file systems with metal racks, each containing 100 or more slides.

Magnifiers When you're looking at slides on a slide sorter or light table, you will need a magnifier (also called a loupe or lupe) in order to evaluate sharpness and detail. The Schneider viewing glass comes in three strengths for 4X, 6X, or 8X magnification. With the 4X magnifier you can see the entire image. The 8X magnifier shows only a portion of the slide.

Projector accessories Slide shows are commonly used in business and entertainment. The easiest way to put together a slide show is to simply talk about the slides as you operate the projector. A more polished presentation can be achieved by taping the narration and sound effects you want and changing slides at appropriate points. But if you want to get more sophisticated, equipment is available which enables you to run completely automated shows using one or more projectors.

For use in automated shows, projectors should focus each slide automatically and have an accessory outlet for sound synchronization. If you want to have one slide dissolve into another in exact registration on the screen, you will need a projector like the Kodak Ektagraphic that has exact horizontal and vertical slide registration.

Automatic timers that change the slides at predetermined intervals are available for use with some projectors. However, many shows require slide changes at varying intervals. In this case, signals recorded on the same tape as the narration activate the slide-changing mechanism. A sound synchronizer, such as the Kodak EC Sound-Slide Synchronizer, is a machine that enables you to record the narration and sound effects on one channel and the slide change signals on another, so the signals aren't audible. During the presentation the synchronizer receives the signal from the tape and activates the slide advance mechanism. You can override the recorded signal with the remote control advance button.

A dissolve unit such as the Kodak EC-K Solid State Dissolve Control coordinates several projectors. It can act as an automatic timer, advancing the slides at regular intervals, or it can allow the slides to advance on a signal from other equipment. By controlling how quickly the slides change, the dissolve unit produces special effects such as superimposed images, one slide dissolving into another, or animated sequences created by rapidly alternating images.

For shows with two or more projectors, there are special tables that hold the projectors one above the other, allowing for registration of images from different projectors.

Welt Safe-Lock, Inc.

Projector screens can be made to hang on the wall. Others, like this SCR screen made by Welt Safe-Lock, have a free-standing collapsible support. There are three kinds of screen surfaces. A glass beaded surface bounces the light back at a narrow angle, producing a very bright image as long as you sit directly in front of it, not off to one side. A silver lenticular screen reflects light at a narrow angle also, and the image is almost as bright as with a glass beaded surface. It intensifies colors and is the best surface to use if the room can't be darkened, but the highlights may look metallic. A mat white screen is the least bright but the image may be viewed from any angle. It is the best kind to use for shows involving more than one projector if you are covering a wide area of screen.

Projectors may have rotary trays, rectangular trays, or slide cubes. Round trays hold eighty or more slides, so they are suited to large shows. Rectangular trays and cubes hold fewer slides but provide more compact slide storage than round trays. Lenses of various focal lengths are available for many projectors and are used when the projector must be much closer to or farther from the screen than normal.

The Kodak Carousel 5200 projector features automatic focusing, remote control, and a built-in screen for previewing slides or showing them to small groups. It also has an illuminated control panel, built-in reading light, and an accessory outlet for sound synchronization.

Courtesy of Eastman Kodak Co.

CUSTOM LAB SERVICES

Many photographers depend on labs to do some or all of their processing and printing. There are two kinds of labs: amateur-market labs do the work when you drop the film off at a drug store, department store, or camera store; custom labs deal directly with you. The quality of the work may be excellent from either, but there are differences in the services they offer.

Amateur-market labs deal primarily in snapshot processing and do much of their work, such as printing and processing, by machine. They offer a limited range of services which generally includes duplicates, enlargements, and photo-greeting cards, and may include some more specialized services as well.

Custom labs deal primarily with photographers who have specific requests about the way they want their film processed or printed. They use machines for some of the work but they offer many services such as cropping, color correction, and retouching that can be done only by people. If you want to go beyond snapshot records and begin to display your prints, you will either want to find a custom lab whose work you like—or learn to do darkroom work yourself.

There are several custom labs that do business by mail. They advertise in popular and professional camera magazines and will send an information packet on request. To find a local custom lab, check your Yellow Pages, ask at a local camera store, or ask a local photographer.

The range of services varies from one lab to the next, and the quality may vary too. Larger labs generally offer most, if not all, of the following services.

	Starting point	Possibilities	
Processing means developing black-and-white or color film to negatives or slides. When processing the film, a lab can push it, that is, increase the normal development time. It is common for photographers shooting in dim light to shoot a roll of film at a higher ASA than that at which the film is rated. As a result, the film is underexposed, and to compensate for this it can be overdeveloped. A pushed negative will not look exactly like one that was normally exposed and developed—grain and contrast usually increase and color balance may shift—but pushing is useful for low-light situations.	Undeveloped film: black-and-white or color	Standard processing	Normal processing resulting in slides or negatives.
		Push processing	Increases film ASA for shooting in low light; data packed with film will indicate if feasible.
Prints Custom labs will make enlarged prints from black-and-white or color negatives or from color slides. They may offer various types and qualities of prints that vary quite a bit in cost. Ask to see examples of different kinds of prints before you make a decision. Cropping and color correction are usually included in the cost of the print.	Negatives: black-and-white or color	Machine prints	Generally the least expensive print. Made by a machine that evaluates density and color balance. Only limited cropping and color balance controls are possible.
		Custom prints	Made by a human operator. Allows for use of custom services such as dodging, burning in, cropping, masking, etc.
	Negatives: color	Dye transfer prints	The most expensive color print process. Requires the use of three color-separated negatives to make the final print.
	Negatives: color or Slides: color	Black-and-white prints	Black-and-white prints may be made from color negatives or slides but gray tones may look different than in a print made from a black-and-white negative.
	Slides: color	Prints	The print is made directly from the slide (without using a negative).
	Slides: black-and-white or color	Internegatives	The slide is enlarged onto negative film and the resulting negative is then used to make an enlarged print. Contrast can be controlled better than with a print made directly from a slide.

	Starting point	Possibilities	
	Slides: black-and-white or color	Enlarged transparencies	Also called display transparencies. The slide is enlarged onto transparency film, 4 x 5 or larger. The resulting image is lit from behind for viewing. Enlarged transparencies are often displayed in light-box frames.
		Duplicates	Cropping, plus some density and color balance correction, can be done in the duplicate.
Proofing Proofs are used to evaluate the pictures and determine which ones to enlarge and what corrections to make in the final printing. Several kinds of proofs are available. What is best for you will depend on how large you want the image to be and whether you want to have the individual proofs corrected for exposure and color.	Negatives: black-and-white or color	Contact proofs	"Gang printed," i.e., usually with the negatives from one roll of film on one piece of paper; all images the same size as the negative. Individual frames are not individually exposed or color corrected.
		Enlarged proofs	All images enlarged but printed on the same sheet of paper. Individual frames are not individually exposed or color corrected.
		Custom proofs, previews	Each image is enlarged by machine and printed on a separate piece of paper. Allows individual exposure and color correction of frames on the roll.
Printing controls When you order prints from negatives or slides, you can request any of the printing adjustments listed below. Some of these "post shooting" controls add to the cost of the print (the first four listed here usually do not), but they can help to achieve the effect you want in the final print.	Dodging		Lightening areas of the print that are too dark.
	Burning in		Darkening areas of the print that are too light.
	Cropping		Printing only part of the image area, usually to eliminate unnecessary elements at the edges.
	Color correction		You can request that specific changes be made in the color balance of the print, or if you are uncertain, ask that the printer use his or her own judgment. Some labs will make a test strip to show you what's possible.
	Masking		Used to control and reduce contrast. It is especially useful for maintaining highlight and shadow detail when the original negative or slide is contrasty.
	Perspective correction		When you tilt the camera to photograph a building, the perspective becomes distorted and the verticals appear to merge toward the top of the picture. Some of this distortion can be corrected by tilting the easel in the opposite direction when printing.
	Superimposition		Printing two images on the same sheet of paper. Often used in wedding photography (the bride and the groom superimposed on an image of the wedding, for example).
	Negative retouching		Usually possible only with 2¼" x 2¼" or larger negatives. Normally used for removing blemishes from portraits.
	Opaquing		Used to eliminate distracting backgrounds and other large areas from the negative.
	Embossed texture		The print surface is actually embossed with a texture such as pebble, silk, or linen.
	Cutout		A cutout is used to block light from the edges of the print so the image takes the shape of a heart, oval, circle, etc.
	Vignetting		A cutout is held in an out-of-focus position during printing so the image blends into the white paper instead of having a clearly delineated edge.
	Texture screens		Placed over the paper at the time the print is made, these screens add a textured pattern to the image. Canvas, linen, and mezzotint are some of the possibilities.
Special services With photographs being used more and more for interior decorating, labs now offer oversized prints, so your photograph can be as large as a painting, or even a mural. Many labs also offer some mounting and framing services.	Murals		Many labs will make murals from slides or negatives in color or black-and-white. Price is usually based on the number of square feet.
	Cards and calendars		Labs often have stock greetings, invitations, or a calendar which they will print alongside your photograph.
	Copy prints		If the original negative has been lost or destroyed, a negative can be made by photographing an existing print. This new negative is then used to make copy prints. Slides can also be made by photographing prints.

GLOSSARY

Prepared by Lista Duren

Aberration Optical defect in a lens (sometimes unavoidable) causing distortion or loss of sharpness in the final image.

Adapter ring A ring used to attach one camera item to another; for example, to attach a lens to a camera in reverse position in order to increase image sharpness when focusing very close to the subject.

Angle of view The amount of a scene that can be recorded by a particular lens; determined by the focal length of the lens.

Aperture The lens opening formed by the iris diaphragm inside the lens. The size is variable and is controlled by the aperture ring on the lens.

Aperture-priority mode An automatic exposure system in which the photographer sets the aperture (f-stop) and the camera selects a shutter speed for correct exposure.

Aperture ring The band on the camera lens that, when turned, adjusts the size of the opening in the iris diaphragm and changes the amount of light that reaches the film.

ASA A number rating that indicates the speed of a film. Stands for American Standards Association.

Auto winder See **Motor drive unit.**

Automatic exposure A mode of camera operation in which the camera automatically adjusts either the aperture, the shutter speed, or both for proper exposure.

Automatic flash An electronic flash unit with a light-sensitive cell that determines the length of the flash for proper exposure by measuring the light reflected back from the subject.

Averaging meter An exposure meter with a wide angle of view. The indicated exposure is based on an average of all the light values in the scene.

Base The supporting material that holds a photographic emulsion. For film, it is plastic or acetate. For prints, it is paper.

Bellows An accordion-pleated section inserted between the lens and the camera body. In close-up photography the bellows allows closer-than-normal focusing resulting in a larger image.

Body The light-tight box that contains the camera mechanisms and protects the film from light until you are ready to make an exposure.

Bounce light Indirect light produced by pointing the light source away from the subject and using a ceiling or other surface to reflect the light back toward the subject. Softer and less harsh than direct light.

Bracketing Taking several photographs of the same scene at different exposure settings, some greater than and some less than the setting indicated by the meter, to ensure a well-exposed photograph.

Built-in meter An exposure meter in the camera that takes a light reading (usually through the camera lens) and relays exposure information to the electronic controls in an automatic camera or to the photographer if the camera is being operated manually.

Cable release An encased wire which attaches at one end to the shutter release on the camera and has a plunger on the other end that the photographer depresses to activate the shutter. Used to avoid camera movement or to activate the shutter from a distance.

Cassette A light-tight metal or plastic container in which 35mm film is packaged.

Center-weighted meter A through-the-lens exposure meter that measures light values from the entire scene but gives greater emphasis to those in the center of the image area.

Close-up A larger-than-normal image obtained by using a lens closer than normal to the subject.

Close-up lens An attachment placed in front of an ordinary lens to allow focusing at a shorter distance in order to increase image size.

Color balance The overall accuracy with which the colors in a color photograph match or are capable of matching those in the original scene. Color films are balanced for use with specific light sources.

Color temperature Description of the color of a light source. Measured on a scale of degrees Kelvin.

Compound lens A lens made up of several lens elements.

Contrast The difference in brightness between the light and dark parts of a scene or photograph.

Contrasty Having greater-than-normal differences between light and dark areas.

Cool Toward the green-blue-violet end of the visible spectrum.

Daylight film Color film that has been balanced to produce natural-looking color when exposed in daylight. Images will look reddish if daylight film is used with tungsten light.

Depth of field The distance between the nearest and farthest points that appear in acceptably sharp focus in a photograph. Depth of field varies with lens aperture, focal length, and camera-to-subject distance.

Diaphragm (iris diaphragm) The mechanism controlling the size of the lens opening and therefore the amount of light that reaches the film. It consists of several overlapping metal leaves inside the lens that form a circular opening of variable sizes. (You can see it as you look into the front of the lens.) The size of the opening is referred to as the f-stop or aperture.

Diffused light Light that has been scattered by reflection or by passing through a translucent material. An even, often shadowless, light.

DIN A number rating used in Europe that indicates the speed of a film. Stands for Deutsche Industrie Norm.

Diopter Unit of measurement that indicates the magnifying power of a close-up lens.

Direct light Light shining directly on the subject and producing strong highlights and deep shadows.

Directional/diffused light Light that is partly direct and partly scattered. Softer and less harsh than direct light.

Electronic flash (strobe) A camera accessory that provides a brilliant flash of light. A battery-powered unit requires occasional recharging or battery replacement, but, unlike a flashbulb, can be used repeatedly.

Emulsion A thin coating of gelatin, containing a light-sensitive material such as silver-halide crystals plus other chemicals, spread evenly on one surface of film or paper to record an image.

Environmental portrait A photograph in which the subject's surroundings are important to the portrait.

Exposure 1. The act of allowing light to strike a light-sensitive surface. 2. The amount of light reaching the film, controlled by the combination of aperture and shutter speed.

Exposure meter (light meter) An instrument that measures the brightness of light and provides aperture and shutter speed combinations for correct exposure. Exposure meters may be built into the camera or they may be separate instruments.

Exposure mode The type of camera operation (such as manual, shutter-priority, aperture-priority) that determines which controls you set and which ones the camera sets automatically. Some cameras operate in only one mode. Others may be used in a variety of modes.

Extension tubes Metal rings attached between the camera lens and the body to allow closer-than-normal focusing in order to increase the image size.

Fill light A light source or reflector used to lighten shadow areas so that contrast is decreased.

Film A roll or sheet of a flexible material coated on one side with a light-sensitive emulsion and used in the camera to record an image.

Film advance lever A device, usually on the top of the camera, that winds the film forward a measured distance so that an unexposed segment moves into place behind the shutter.

Film plane (focal plane) The surface inside the camera on which the image is in sharp focus.

Film speed The relative sensitivity to light of photographic film. Measured by ASA (or ISO or DIN) rating. Faster film (higher number) is more sensitive to light and requires less exposure than slower film.

Filter A piece of colored glass or plastic placed in front of the camera lens to alter the quality of the light reaching the film.

Filter factor A number, provided by the filter manufacturer, that tells you how much to increase exposure to compensate for the light absorbed by the filter. You usually don't have to be concerned with filter factors if your camera has a through-the-lens metering system.

Fisheye lens An extreme wide angle lens covering a 180° angle of view. Straight lines appear curved at the edge of the photograph, and the image itself may be circular.

Flare Stray light that reflects between the lens surfaces and results in a loss of contrast or an overall grayness in the final image.

Flash 1. A short burst of light emitted by a flashbulb or electronic flash unit at the same time the film is exposed. 2. The equipment used to produce this light.

Flashbulb A battery-powered bulb that emits one bright flash of light and then must be replaced.

Flat Having less-than-normal differences between light and dark areas.

Focal length The distance from the optical center of the lens to the film plane when the lens is focused on infinity. The focal length is usually expressed in millimeters (mm) and determines the angle of view (how much of the scene can be included in the picture) and the size of objects in the image. A 100mm lens, for example, has a narrow angle of view and magnifies objects by comparison with a lens of shorter focal length.

Focal plane See **Film plane.**

Focus 1. The point at which the rays of light coming through the lens converge to form a sharp image. The picture is "in focus" or sharpest when this point coincides with the film plane. 2. To change the lens-to-film distance (or the camera-to-subject distance) until the image is sharp.

Focusing ring The band on the camera lens that, when turned, moves the lens in relation to the film plane, focusing the camera for specific distances.

Focusing screen See **Viewing screen.**

Frame 1. A single image in a roll of film. 2. The edges of an image.

Fresnel An optical surface with concentric circular steps. Used in a viewing screen to equalize the brightness of the image.

F-stop (f-number) A numerical designation (f/2, f/2.8, etc.) indicating the size of the aperture (lens opening).

Ghosting Bright spots in the picture the same shape as the aperture (lens opening) caused by reflections between lens surfaces.

Grain The speckled effect caused by particles of silver clumping together in the negative.

Guide number A number on a flash unit that can be used to calculate the correct aperture for a particular film speed and flash-to-subject distance.

Hand-held meter An exposure meter that is separate from the camera.

Hand hold To support the camera with the hands rather than with a tripod or other fixed support.

High-contrast film Film that records light tones lighter and dark tones darker than normal, thereby increasing the difference between tones.

Hot shoe A clip on the top of the camera that attaches a flash unit and provides an electrical link to synchronize the flash with the camera shutter, eliminating the need for a sync cord.

Hyperfocal distance The distance to the nearest object in focus when the lens is focused on infinity. Setting the lens to focus on this distance instead of on infinity will keep the farthest objects in focus as well as extend the depth of field to include objects closer to the camera.

Incident-light meter A hand-held exposure meter that measures the amount of light falling on the subject. See also **Reflected-light meter.**

Indoor film See **Tungsten film.**

Infinity designated ∞. The farthest distance marked on the focusing ring of the lens, generally about 50 feet. When the camera is focused on infinity, all objects at that distance or farther away will be sharp.

Infrared film Film that is sensitive to wavelengths slightly longer than those in the visible spectrum as well as to some wavelengths within the visible spectrum.

Interchangeable lens A lens that can be removed from the camera and replaced by another lens.

Iris diaphragm See **Diaphragm.**

ISO A film speed rating that is replacing the ASA and DIN ratings. Stands for International Standards Organization.

Latitude The amount of over- or under-exposure possible without a significant change in the quality of the image.

LED See **Light-emitting diode.**

Lens One or more pieces of optical glass used in the camera to gather and focus light rays to form an image.

Lens cleaning fluid A liquid made for cleaning lenses without damaging the delicate coating on the lens surface.

Lens coating A thin transparent coating on the surface of the lens which reduces light reflections.

Lens element A single piece of optical glass that acts as a lens or as part of a lens.

Lens hood (lens shade) A shield that fits around the lens to prevent extraneous light from entering the lens and causing ghosting or flare.

Lens tissue A soft lint-free tissue made specifically for cleaning camera lenses. Not the same as eyeglass cleaning tissue.

Light-emitting diode (LED) A display of colored lights in the viewfinder of some cameras that gives you information about aperture and shutter speed settings or other exposure data.

Light meter See **Exposure meter.**

Long-focal-length lens (telephoto lens) A lens that provides a narrow angle of view of a scene, including less of a scene than a lens of normal focal length and therefore magnifying objects in the image.

Macro lens A lens specifically designed for close-up photography and capable of good optical performance when used very close to a subject.

Macrophotography Production of images on film that are life-size or larger.

Magnification The size of an object as it appears in an image. Magnification of an image on film is determined by the lens focal length. A long-focal-length lens makes an object appear larger (provides greater magnification) than a short-focal-length lens.

Main light The primary source of illumination.

Manual exposure A nonautomatic mode of camera operation in which the photographer sets both the aperture and the shutter speed.

Match-needle metering A manual exposure mode in which the photographer adjusts the shutter speed and aperture until the camera's viewfinder shows (by matching two needles or by other indicators) that the film will be properly exposed.

Matte Not shiny.

Meter 1. See **Exposure meter.** 2. To take a light reading with a meter.

Mirror A polished metallic reflector set inside the camera body at a 45° angle to the lens to reflect the image up onto the focusing screen. When a picture is taken, the mirror moves so that light can reach the film.

Motor drive unit (auto winder) A camera accessory that automatically advances the film once it has been exposed.

Negative 1. An image with colors or dark and light tones that are the opposite of those in the original scene. 2. Film that was exposed in the camera and processed to form a negative image.

Negative film Photographic film that produces a negative image upon exposure and development.

Neutral density filter A piece of dark glass or plastic placed in front of the camera lens to decrease the intensity of light entering the lens. It affects exposure, but not color.

Normal-focal-length lens (standard lens) A lens that provides about the same angle of view of a scene as the human eye and that does not unduly magnify or diminish the relative size of objects in the image.

Open up To increase the size of the lens aperture. The opposite of stop down.

Orthochromatic film Film that is sensitive to blue and green light but not red light.

Overexposure Exposing the film to more light than is needed to render the scene as the eye sees it. Results in a negative that is too dark (dense) or a positive that is too light.

Pan To move the camera during the exposure in the same direction as a moving subject. The effect is that the subject stays relatively sharp and the background becomes blurred.

Panchromatic film Film that is sensitive to the wavelengths of the visible spectrum.

Pentaprism A five-sided optical device used in an eye-level viewfinder to correct the image from the focusing screen so that it appears right side up and correct left to right.

Perspective The illusion of a three-dimensional space suggested primarily by converging lines and the decrease in size of objects farther from the camera.

Photoflood A tungsten lamp designed especially for use in photographic studios. It emits light at 3400 K and is suitable for use with tungsten Type A film.

Photomicrography Photographing through a microscope.

Polarizing screen (polarizing filter) A filter placed in front of the camera lens to reduce reflections from nonmetallic surfaces like glass or water.

Positive An image with colors or light and dark tones that are similar to those in the original scene.

Print An image (usually a positive one) on photographic paper, made from a negative or a transparency.

Quartz lamp A tungsten lamp which has high intensity, small size, long life, and constant color temperature. Balanced for use with tungsten film.

Reciprocity effect (reciprocity failure) A shift in the color balance or the darkness of an image caused by very long or very short exposures.

Reflected-light meter An exposure meter (hand held or built into the camera) that reads the amount of light reflected from the subject. See also **Incident-light meter.**

Reflector Any surface—a ceiling, a card, an umbrella, etc.—used to bounce light onto a subject.

Reversal film Photographic film that produces a positive image (a transparency) upon exposure and development.

Reversal processing A procedure for producing a positive image on film (a transparency) from the film exposed in the camera or a positive print from a transparency with no negative involved.

Rewind crank A device, usually on the top of the camera, for winding the film back into the cassette once it has been exposed.

Shoe A clip on a camera for attaching a flash unit. See also **Hot shoe.**

Short-focal-length lens (wide-angle lens) A lens that provides a wide angle of view of a scene, including more of the subject area than a lens of normal focal length.

Shutter A device in the camera that opens and closes to expose the film to light for a measured length of time.

Shutter-priority mode An automatic exposure system in which the photographer sets the shutter speed and the camera selects the aperture (f-stop) for correct exposure.

Shutter release The mechanism, usually a button on the top of the camera, that activates the shutter to expose the film.

Shutter speed dial The camera control that selects the length of time the film is exposed to light.

Silhouette A dark shape with little or no detail appearing against a light background.

Single-lens-reflex (SLR) A type of camera with one lens which is used both for viewing and for taking the picture. A mirror inside the camera reflects the image up into the viewfinder. When the picture is taken, this mirror moves out of the way, allowing the light entering the lens to travel directly to the film.

Slide See **transparency.**

SLR See **single-lens-reflex.**

Spectrum The range of radiant energy from extremely short wavelengths to extremely long ones. The visible spectrum includes only the wavelengths to which the human eye is sensitive.

Speed 1. The relative ability of a lens to transmit light. Measured by the largest aperture at which the lens can be used. A fast lens has a larger maximum aperture and can transmit more light than a slow one. 2. The relative sensitivity to light of photographic film. See **Film speed.**

Standard lens See **Normal-focal-length lens.**

Spot meter An exposure meter with a narrow angle of view, used to take a reading from a small portion of the scene being photographed.

Stop 1. An aperture setting that indicates the size of the lens opening. 2. A change in exposure by a factor of two. Changing the aperture from one setting to the next doubles or halves the amount of light reaching the film. Changing the shutter speed from one setting to the next does the same thing. Either changes the exposure one stop.

Stop down To decrease the size of the lens aperture. The opposite of open up.

Stopped-down automatic exposure A mode of operation possible with some cameras. Ordinarily the camera meters the scene (and you view the scene) with the aperture wide open, stopping down to the proper aperture only when the picture is taken. In stopped-down exposure the camera meters the scene with the aperture already stopped down.

Strobe See **Electronic flash.**

Substitution reading An exposure meter reading taken from something other than the subject, such as a gray card of standard darkness or the photographer's hand.

Sync (or synchronization) cord An electrical wire that links a flash unit to a camera's shutter release mechanism.

Synchronize To cause a flash unit to fire while the camera shutter is open.

Telephoto lens See **long-focal-length lens.**

35mm The width of the film used in all the cameras described in this book.

Through-the-lens meter (TTL meter) An exposure meter built into the camera which takes light readings through the lens.

Transparency (slide) A positive image on a clear film base viewed by passing light through from behind with a projector or light box. Usually in color.

Tripod A three-legged support for the camera.

TTL Abbreviation for through the lens, as in through-the-lens viewing or metering.

Tungsten-balanced film Color film that has been balanced to produce colors that look natural when exposed in tungsten light, specifically light of 3200 K color temperature. Images will look bluish if tungsten-balanced film is used in daylight. *Type A tungsten film* has a slightly different balance for use with photoflood bulbs of 3400 K color temperature.

Umbrella reflector An apparatus constructed like a parasol with a reflective surface on the inside. Used to bounce or diffuse light onto a subject.

Underexposure Exposing the film to less light than is needed to render the scene as the eye sees it. Results in a negative that is too light (thin) or a positive that is too dark.

Viewfinder eyepiece An opening in the camera through which the photographer can see the scene to be photographed.

Viewing screen The surface on which the image in the camera appears for viewing. This image appears upside down and reversed left to right unless the camera contains a pentaprism to correct it.

Vignette To shade the edges of an image so they are underexposed. A lens hood that is too long for the lens will cut into the angle of view and cause vignetting.

Visible spectrum See **Spectrum.**

Warm Toward the red-orange-yellow end of the visible spectrum.

Wide-angle distortion Unusual changes in perspective or in the appearance of objects caused by using a wide-angle (short-focal-length) lens very close to the subject.

Wide-angle lens See **Short-focal-length lens.**

Zone focusing Presetting the focus to photograph action so that the entire area in which the action may take place will be sharp.

Zoom lens A lens with several moving elements which can be used to produce a continuous range of focal lengths.

INDEX